THE SPIRIT OF
Soul Food

The Spirit of Soul Food

RACE, FAITH, AND FOOD JUSTICE

CHRISTOPHER CARTER

UNIVERSITY OF
ILLINOIS PRESS
Urbana, Chicago, and Springfield

Library of Congress Cataloging-in-Publication Data
Names: Carter, Christopher, 1981– author.
Title: The spirit of soul food: race, faith, and food
    justice / Christopher Carter.
Description: Urbana, Chicago: University of
    Illinois Press, [2021] | Includes bibliographical
    references and index.
Identifiers: LCCN 2021015717 (print) | LCCN
    2021015718 (ebook) | ISBN 9780252044120
    (cloth: acid-free paper) | ISBN 9780252086175
    (paperback: acid-free paper) | ISBN
    9780252053061 (ebook)
Subjects: LCSH: Food—Religious aspects—
    Christianity. | Food supply—Religious aspects—
    Christianity. | United States—Population
    policy. | Population policy—Religious aspects—
    Christianity. | African American cooking.
Classification: LCC BR115.N87 C375 2021 (print) |
    LCC BR115.N87 (ebook) | DDC 261.8/5—dc23
LC record available at https://lccn.loc.gov/
    2021015717
LC ebook record available at https://lccn.loc.gov/
    2021015718

This book is dedicated to my grandfather Robert Martin, whose stories of survival are woven throughout this text; my mother, Elaine Brown, who showed me how to make a way out of no way; my wife, Gabrielle, whose faith in me sustained me during periods of doubt; and my son, Isaiah, for whom I long to make this world a better place.

Contents

Preface

I did not want to write this book.

Perhaps this is an odd way to start a book that you have been working on for almost six years, odd but honest. Christianity, food justice, and food sovereignty are intertwined in my family history, and as far as I can remember, I believed there was a moral obligation to provide access to food for all people. This moral obligation is seemingly apparent to Black, Indigenous, and other people of color whose ancestors lived in the shadow of hunger and who currently live behind the veil of cheap food that is dependent upon the exploitation of our labor.

In earlier drafts of this book, I hid my ethical commitment to what I refer to as "soulfull" eating behind this moral obligation. I assumed (or hoped) that all I needed to do was to make a clear and logical argument that led the reader to conclude—as I had—that as the best practice of soulfull eating, black veganism (which I will define and describe in the introduction) and the pursuit of food sovereignty should become a spiritual practice among Black Christians and within Black churches and communities. I assumed that if I presented facts and data that revealed how much Black, Indigenous, other people of color, and the poor suffer from food apartheid and environmental racism and are the victims of land theft, then my prescriptions for the creation of food-sovereign communities around church land would be readily accepted, if not adopted, by some communities.

However, for Black folks, those of us descended from enslaved Africans whom European Christian men purchased in part because of their agricultural and culinary acumen, facts and data can only take us so far. And rightly so. Our foodways are an expression of our identity, a way of maintaining connections to our ancestors and our ancestral homelands; our foodways are personal and communal, emotional and habitual. In order for my community to take my work seriously I need to wrestle the culinary deity that soul food has become. I need to be transparent about my dietary conversion and the challenge of maintaining an identity that is found in our mothers' pots, our grandmothers' gardens, and the backbreaking labor of our enslaved ancestors if I expect this work to have any tangible impact beyond the hallways of academic institutions.

That is why I did not want to write *this* book.

Doing so would require me to be culturally vulnerable—to yet again have my "authenticity" questioned. Soul food, like jazz, is a Black, American, and southern invention. For countless other Black people and myself, soul food is a source from which we derive essential character traits that remind us of who we are and inspire whom we want to become. Given this, why would anyone write a book that argues for the reimagination of what soul food ought to be?

I believe that is what our ancestors would do—I believe that given the devastating impact that our current food system has on Black folk, they would have done their best to change their consumption and provision of food in order to survive and ensure the survival of future generations.

My gym membership has become my monthly reminder that change is never easy. The difficulty of change is especially true concerning the relationships we develop around food. If soul food is an indelible part of Black culture and identity, an identity that has been and continues to be under constant pressure to conform to the white racial imagination, then one must be careful and acknowledge these realities when arguing for the reimagination of Black foodways. One must take seriously the realities of what it means to live in a society that is founded upon anti-Black racism and that actively seeks to "white-wash" Black history and ignore or take credit for Black culinary and agricultural ingenuity. These historical traumas suggest that if one desires to examine the theoethical, racial, culinary, agricultural, and spiritual dimensions of soul food in such a way that Black folks *feel heard*, then one's examination should be guided by the Christian call of radical compassion.

Compassion both informs and shapes my exploration and reimagination of Black foodways; this approach too remained hidden from the reader in earlier drafts of this book. All too often compassion is misunderstood or misrepresented as sentiment, and the last thing I wanted anyone to think about my examination of food injustice, racism, and colonialism was that I was sentimental. However, my colleague Dr. Seth Schoen helped me realize that compassion informs my person so much so that my not mentioning it does not result in it being absent from the text.[1] Rather, not being transparent to my commitment to radical compassion obscures my argument and suppresses a critical part of who I know myself to be. I was reminded that compassion, properly understood, always promotes actions that lead to the restoration and flourishing of all people, especially those who suffer under the yoke of structural evil.

The ethic of compassion—to love God and neighbor, to do unto others as we would have them do unto us—is the essence of how Christians are called to practice Christianity. This form of compassion is radical because it is the ground from which those of us who are Christian, following the example set by Jesus, nonviolently resist empire by cultivating relationships built on love, justice, and accountability with God, ourselves, and our neighbors. Frank Rogers suggests that Jesus's spiritual path of radical compassion has three dimensions: "a deepening of our connection to the compassion of God, a restoration to a humanity fully loved and alive, and an increase to our capacity to be instruments of compassion toward others in the world."[2] These three dimensions inform my proposal that a decolonial theological anthropology—that is, a theoethical way of being human that resists the dehumanizing logic of Enlightenment colonial thinking—should be the basis for the reimagination of what soul food should look like.

The religion of Jesus in the Gospels is a spiritual path developed by a Palestinian Jew in response to the colonizing forces of the Roman Empire. The Gospel narratives present us with a decolonial spirituality rooted in radical compassion that resists evil with weapons of love and dignity and not with hate or the submissive endurance that is often attributed to Christian nonviolent resistance movements. Jesus's method of resisting social and structural evil models a third way of being in the world, a way that is not rooted in hate (fight) or submission (flight); instead, it centers on reclaiming one's dignity. The three eating practices that I propose (soulfull eating, seeking justice for food workers, and caring for the earth) embody Jesus's third way of being in the world and focus on reclaiming our culinary, agricultural, and human dignity as Black people from racist ideologies and colonial anthropologies that have misshapen our relationship with food and the land.

As a social ethicist and practical theologian, I am committed to beginning my theoethical analysis where people are. I examine what people do in order to discern what they believe, and typically this leads to identifying a gap between stated belief and actual practice. *Our humanness lies in this gap.* Our hope for who we long to become and our fear of becoming the dehumanizing evil that we long to dismantle lie in the gap between what we say we believe and what our actions demonstrate that we believe. Because soul food sits at the intersection of so many religious and cultural signifiers for Black people, soul food represents hope for some, fear for others, and a combination of the two for most of us. Compassion enables us to explore the complexities of Black culinary and agricultural history without resorting to dehumanizing stereotypes or victim-blaming people of African descent. My hope is that viewing Black foodways through the lens of compassion will enable you, the reader, to begin to understand why Black culinary identity is vital to Black folks and how our plates and bowls became complex and contested sites since our enslavement.

Food matters to African Americans because it is an essential means by which everyday Black folk construct our narratives of who we are. The power to tell our stories and define ourselves through what we consume is precisely why our foodways must be consistently examined. How are the stories we tell ourselves about traditional notions of soul food still useful? Are these stories tied to certain foods? Is the idea of soul food more about the foods themselves or the wisdom of the communities that created these foods? Given the structural racism within the US food system and my moral obligation to practice an antioppressive liberative Christianity, how might soul food be used to tell stories about whom we want to become and not only of who we once were?

My pursuit of answering the last question has led me to an unexpected place: soulfull eating, specifically, black veganism. If food is a means by which we can tell our stories, and if the stories that we want to tell ourselves and our communities about Black survival, self-determination, and flourishing are built upon a foundation of Black resistance to oppression, then reimagining soul food through the practice of black veganism seems like a logical conclusion.

But as we have already discussed, what we choose to eat is not merely a logical decision; it is a product of our identity, spirituality, and affective relationships within our communities. The challenge in answering questions about Black foodways and forming an ethical vision of what soul food should become is that these questions require us to go deep. We must delve deep into the trauma of enslavement and exploitation, deep into the wounds tied to our struggle to own and keep land. We must become a healing balm to the sorrow of our ancestors. We must allow ourselves to be healed, for our sake and for the sake of our children. The story of soul food must remain a story of resistance, resilience, community, and empowerment. This book is just one new chapter in the beautiful story of soul food.

THE SPIRIT OF
Soul Food

Introduction

Knowing, Eating, and Believing

What comes to mind when you hear the words "soul food"? Do the words make you hungry and cause your mouth to water? Or do you visualize foods that are associated with soul food: red beans and rice, fried chicken, baked macaroni and cheese, collard greens, and cornbread? Or do the words "soul food" bring to mind special occasions when family, friends, and play cousins gather to break bread, tell jokes, and play spades? For Black folks, some or all of these things can come to mind when we think about soul food because soul food has always signified more than just a cuisine.

Soul food—the cuisine of formerly enslaved African American and African diasporic peoples in the southern United States—is as much about how foods are grown and cooked and Black culture as it is a culinary description. As a child and young adult, I never thought much of or about the term. For me, soul food was just "food"; it's what we ate after church, on holidays or special occasions, or on Tuesday. It's not that I didn't know that there was something special or unique about what we ate and how we prepared it. I grew up in West Michigan and had a diverse group of friends; I ate at enough white people's houses to know that our food tasted *very* different, even if we were eating the same foods. But what exactly made the food prepared by my parents and grandparents so different? Was this difference limited to the way the food was seasoned and prepared, or was there something more significant?

KNOWING

Who cooked the best dish? There was always an unofficial/official competition to prepare the dish that everyone would compliment the most while we were eating. When the conversation turned to comparing the various foods against one another, it tended to flow from recipes and ingredients to stories about how these recipes were passed down from our elders. Eventually, someone would talk about how these foods helped our ancestors during their enslavement and Jim and Jane Crow. These foods contained painful, powerful, and empowering memories of Black suffering and self-determination. The family elders would explain that we eat chitlins because we were given the scraps of domestic animals, and we needed to find a way to make all the parts palatable. And this was why there was always some sort of pork in the greens, because it was likely all the protein the slaves would be able to eat. Black people were forced to make the best out of the worst, and this improvisational ability is how we survived. Our ancestors ate what we now call soul food in order to preserve their communities and promote their flourishing. These myths were etched into my identity, and I was proud to have come from people whose culinary habits reflect our ability to "make a way out of no way."

The history and development of soul food in the United States form a window into the legacy of racism that is tied to the development of industrial agriculture and our current domestic food system. The diets of my Black ancestors were forced upon them by white people who had grown numb to their own evildoing. Forcing Black people to eat food that you would not eat in ways that you would not eat it is racist and dehumanizing. The idea to describe Black cuisine as soul food emerged during the civil rights movement as a way to reclaim a culinary identity based on principles that critique the white racist imagination projected upon Black people and their diets. Soul food is, among other things, an antiracist response to anti-Black racism and its impact on Black foodways—the intersection of Black food and culture.

The shadow of racism, particularly anti-Black and anti-Indigenous, is long-reaching and is evidenced in the development and sustainability of the US domestic food system. The genocidal military conquest of the Americas and subsequent government treaties affected fifteen million

Indigenous people (most of whom were farmers) and resulted in the confiscation of Indigenous land by European and European American settlers. The enslavement of African peoples gave the United States an unpaid, highly skilled labor force to work the land. The post–Civil War food system was built upon Jim and Jane Crow segregation laws that allowed for the economic marginalization of Black farmers and Black domestic workers. The racist foundation of our food system is visible today in the economic exploitation of both traditional farm and factory farm laborers, who are predominantly people of color; the systematic elimination of Black farmland due to an obstructionist US Department of Agriculture; and housing discrimination, which laid the groundwork for food insecurity for Black, Indigenous, and other people of color. Yet despite the ways in which anti-Black racism has made and continues to make the dietary options of all Black people more complicated, we persist toward our collective goal of living a flourishing life.

The genesis of Black American foodways was the survival and pres-ervation of the Black community, and soul food has played a critical role in preserving Black history and culinary genius. When I learned this history, I gained crucial contextual background to the develop-ment of Black foodways in general and soul food in particular. Once I understood the story of soul food, I understood why we have a respon-sibility to find our place within and contribute to this story, *our story*. If soul food is to be a response to food injustice in the Black community, given the myriad of ways industrial agriculture harms Black people—economically, environmentally, ideologically—what should soul food look like today?

This book attempts to do two things in seeking to answer that ques-tion. First, this book argues that Black churches and Black Christians especially, but all Christians in general, should view food justice as an essential aspect of Christian social justice practice. As an act of justice, I suggest that Black people should purchase and consume foods that preserve and promote the flourishing of Black people and other people of color. Borrowing the definition of food justice from food justice activists Robert Gottlieb and Anupama Joshi, I use food justice to mean a state wherein "the benefits and risks of where, what, and how food is grown and produced, transported and distributed,

and accessed and eaten are shared fairly."[1] I will describe how racism
and coloniality, understood as the logic, culture, and structure of our
Eurocentric modern world system, have long been controlling factors
in the development of US food policy. I will also explain how the food
we eat, grow, and distribute is a social justice issue that disproportionately harms Black people specifically and people of color in general,
the global poor, and our planet.

The second goal of the book and my impetus for writing it was to
answer the aforementioned question: What should soul food look like
for Black folks today? Personally, I wanted to explore how my diet could
reflect my cultural identity as an African American and be consistent
with the principal values of my Christian faith: love, justice, and solidarity with the marginalized. In answering these questions, I conclude
this book by constructing a Christian ethical response to the structural
evil that upholds our food system. Our ancestors ate what they had to
eat in order to survive, but the racialized context we currently occupy
is different from theirs in important ways. Neoliberalism and global-
ization are contemporary manifestations of the previous exploitative
economic systems. Given this, how might we learn from our collective
past in order to discern what our contemporary diet ought to be, given
the consequences faced by Black, Indigenous, and other people of
color due to the changes in our food system?

This book is not an attempt to redeem soul food from its critics.
Instead, it is my attempt to reimagine what soul food can be for those
of us who want to eat in a way that is consistent with our theological and
social values and those of us who find parts of our identity baked into
the memory of the foods that remind us of our community. Racism is
in the foundation of US social, political, and economic systems. The
dehumanizing logic of colonialism normalized Indigenous genocide,
African enslavement, and white supremacy. Black foodways and soul
food emerged from within this hostile space. As a result, we should
not be surprised that soul food would be met with criticism, because
by its very nature soul food pushes against the colonial worldview of
white dominance. Soul food tells a different story of Black enslavement
and resistance, a story that prioritizes African history, Black culture,
self-determination, improvisation, and survival. This story does not
conform to the imaginative ways that the dominant European American culture chooses to remember slavery and the Old South. Preserv-

ing Black foodways is important to Black people because it is one way we tell our story, our history on the American continent, on our own terms.

Food justice should be significant to Black people due to the negative impact the US food system has on Black people and Black communities. Indeed, *food should be a part of our conversations when discussing race and racism,* given the links between access to food and the overall health and wellness of Black communities.[2] A significant threat to the broader Black community's ability to live a flourishing life comes from our food supply in the form of highly processed foods, the abundance of fast-food restaurants in Black communities, and the minimally regulated chemical additives that are found in these foods. Unsurprisingly, then, the rates of diet-related disease break down dramatically along racial lines. Food justice is one of the best mechanisms we can use to begin addressing such issues.

Black health and wellness are interconnected with the quest for food justice for our communities. Statistically, Black Americans get sick at younger ages, have more severe illnesses, and die sooner than white Americans.[3] According to the *American Journal of Public Health,* Blacks are 50 percent more likely than whites to experience health problems due to stress.[4] The Centers for Disease Control and Prevention (CDC) reports that Black people are 51 percent more likely to be obese, and half of the Black children born in the United States in the year 2000 are expected to develop type 2 diabetes.[5] Black people are also twice as likely to die from heart disease or stroke than whites.[6] I agree with food justice activist Kristin Wartman that "just as our economy has become starkly stratified with wealth concentrated at the top, it is increasingly clear that we live in a two-tiered food system in which the wealthy tend to eat well and are rewarded with better health, while the poor tend to eat low-quality diets, causing their health to suffer."[7] Given that such health disparities can be traced back to food accessibility within Black communities, food justice should be viewed as essential for the preservation and flourishing of Black people.

EATING

Thursday, November 23, 2006, was my last large family meal before I left Michigan to move to California for graduate school. It's also the last family meal I had before my eating habits changed. My wife and I were hosting Thanksgiving that year, and she spent weeks preparing shopping lists and decorating. She also spent time learning recipes from the cooks in my family; collard greens, cornbread dressing, and sweet potato pie were among the ones I deemed essential for her to learn. At this time I was still a novice in the kitchen, and I didn't trust that I could replicate the recipes nearly as well as she could. I knew it would be a few years before we could afford to come back home, and I wanted to ensure that I would be able to taste home, even if my eyes would not be able to see it.

The word "disconnected" almost seems inadequate when describing how I felt during my first few years in California. When we are lonely or missing our community, being able to eat something that tastes like home goes a long way in helping us remember what it feels like to be "us." There is an affective dimension to food that we all intuitively understand. Eating can be a contemplative experience. Ancestral dishes can remind us of what is real, true, and sacred in our lives. The affective dimension of food can help people feel connected to their communities despite being thousands of miles apart.

I learned of this connection by listening to my maternal grandparents; specifically, my grandfather told me stories about his upbringing in Brookhaven, Mississippi, during Jim Crow. Grandpa Robert is the third out of five children and grew up in an era when poor Black children had to work and help support the family rather than go to school. And work he did. Robert was a farmworker. He picked cotton, berries, and fruit, detasseled corn, plowed fields—he did whatever he could get hired to do. He started working when he was eight years old and subsequently left school to work full time when he was ten. When he was thirteen, Robert left home and became a migrant worker, picking up jobs in Mississippi and Louisiana as he was able and returning home to Brookhaven, often by hitch-hiking, when he knew he would be without work for several weeks.

This life was as difficult as you might be imagining it to be. He told stories of sleeping in run-down cabins that were so drafty he felt as though he was sleeping outside, of finding snakes in the pile of straw that was supposed to be his "bed" while he was working one job. He talked about how important it was to always have savings, because if something went wrong at your job, you were likely to get blamed because you were Black. Once he even worked for a white man who openly let other people refer to my grandfather as the white man's "ni**er"—my grandfather didn't work for that white man too long. Yet despite his difficult childhood, during which he suffered from racism, poverty, and economic exploitation, sometimes he would end these stories by saying that his early life wasn't that bad—"could have been worse" was his response.

What's worse than growing up in conditions that are eerily similar to the Reconstruction Era United States? Death and hunger. Several of my grandfather's friends didn't make it to adulthood, and while he has never said that any of his friends were lynched, lynching is the one topic that he refuses to discuss with anyone. He believes that his work on farms is the reason why he rarely suffered from food insecurity. As taxing as agricultural work was, he loved it. He loved being outside, growing food, farming, and being in nature. People who moved to the city could not afford enough land to grow food on, and for this reason he has always lived in small towns. When my grandfather moved to Three Rivers, Michigan, and bought his first house, one of the first things he did was to plant what he called a garden and what hipsters would probably call a homestead. I grew up spending summers in the country with my grandparents and hearing these stories. I learned to appreciate how hard it was to grow food, how much better food tastes when it is fresh, and how much harder Black people have to work just to afford to be poor.

Our stories are never really our own stories. They are a compilation of our memories, our dreams, and the stories that have been shared with us from our community. As much as my grandfather's story is his story, it is also a part of my own. When I began learning about the exploitation of farmworkers in Central California I felt my grandfather's pain, the literal pain in his back that he suffers from as a result of his years as a farmworker. When I read Marjorie Spiegel's *The Dreaded Comparison: Human and Animal Slavery*, my gut was wrenched by horror.[8] The connection between these sufferings was growing more evident to me every day. Like most (if not all) Black people, I would feel anger and disgust when we were described as behaving "like animals" or were portrayed using simian imagery such as a monkey.

Up until this time in my life I had failed to make the connection between nonhuman animal suffering and Black suffering. From the time of the colonial encounter with Indigenous peoples and the enslavement of Africans as chattel, any living being that wasn't racialized as a white man was considered subhuman and, therefore, could be exploited as needed for the benefit and maintenance of white dominance. The reasoning that the dominant white culture used to justify the racist exploitation of my grandfather and his peers was the same reasoning that was used to justify the exploitation and mistreatment of nonhuman animals and nonhuman nature: a racist hierarchical anthropocentrism where one's moral worth is tied to one's humanness, and one's humanness is determined primarily by one's whiteness or ability to master white performativity.

Anti-Black racism and the human/animal tension are inextricably linked. Throughout this book, I will explain how the structural effects of white supremacy render it impossible for Black people to be seen as full human beings within our current neocolonial social order no matter how well versed we are at performing whiteness. Rather than ignoring the question of the animal as one way to assert our full humanity and demand justice (i.e., I am not an animal, I am human!), I will argue that racism cannot be sufficiently understood without careful analysis of the human/animal tension and that the logic of racism cannot be sufficiently deconstructed without attending to the exploitation of nonhuman animals and nature.

If soul food is understood as a way to respond to anti-Black racism and its impact on Black foodways, and if soul food is supposed to be about the preservation and promotion of the Black community, then those of us who cook and eat soul food must also wrestle with the human/animal tension if soul food is to maintain its place as a source of Black identity, solidarity, and resistance. This realization has led to me abstaining from eating animals and animal products as best as I can and to argue that Black people and especially Black Christians ought to practice what Black feminist writers and sisters Aph Ko and Syl Ko call "black veganism," which I will describe later in this chapter and refer to throughout the book.[9]

I believe that it is a natural human tendency to want to be a part of something larger than ourselves and that this desire helps us find meaning and relevance in our lives. Soul food is one way, a fundamental way, that Black people have been able to feel a sense of kinship with other Black people. Soul food reminds Black people what it feels like to be "us" and to be in love with "us." Admittedly, bridging the gap between practicing black veganism and feeling connected to and accepted within the broader Black community is both an elusive and principal aim in writing this book. However, if soul food is to remain an essential part of the Black experience, as I believe it should, then Black communities must turn inward to examine if the ways we practice being human and our foodways advance us toward the antioppression, antiracist society we hope and work toward.

BELIEVING

The Black Lives Matter movement began in 2013 in response to the acquittal of George Zimmerman of the murder of an unarmed seventeen-year-old African American young man named Trayvon Martin. It was the visionary idea of three radical Black organizers, Alicia Garza, Patrisse Cullors, and Opal Tometi, to create an explicitly Black-centered political movement that would have the will to resist the unjust dehumanization of Black bodies. They describe Black Lives Matter "an ideological and political intervention in a world where Black lives are systematically and intentionally targeted for demise. It is an affirmation of Black folks' humanity, our contributions to this society, and our resilience in the face of deadly oppression."[10]

The Black Lives Matter movement has done outstanding work in arguing for the value of Black lives and pushing society to recognize the wanton disregard for Black life by police officers and other so-called vigilantes. There is a long history of dismissing Black life and reducing Black bodies to objects with only transactional value. The reduction of bodies (Black or otherwise) from subjects to objects has been used to rationalize all manner of exploitation. The history of Western Europe and European settler colonists also reveals that the Christian theology of the European settlers played a key role in normalizing this exploitation by theologically justifying these exploitative practices.

Despite the colonial legacy of American Christianity, among African Americans, religion—particularly Christianity—is likely a part of their lives and the lives of members of their communities. This is the primary reason why I am using Christian theology and ethics to address our food system. While the importance of religion among white people is declining in the United States, according to a recent survey by the Pew Forum, a different picture emerges within African American communities. The survey found that African Americans "are markedly more religious on a variety of measures than the US population as a whole, including the level of affiliation with a religion, attendance at religious services, and the frequency of prayer and religion's importance in life."[11] Approximately 79 percent of African Americans are members of an evangelical, mainline, Catholic, or historically Black Protestant church.[12] The data also show that African Americans are 87 percent more likely to be affiliated with religious groups than other racial/ethnic groups, and nearly 80 percent of African Americans believe that religion is very important in their lives, compared to 56 percent of US adults in general. Religion is such a vital part of the African American community that 76 percent of those who identify as unaffiliated with a particular faith tradition still believe that "religion plays at least a somewhat important role in their lives," and 45 percent of unaffiliated African Americans believe that religion is "very important in their lives."[13]

Given that 79 percent of African Americans identify as Christian, using Christian theological and ethical sources strengthens my argument within the African American community. Additionally, Black churches have at times displayed the capacity to serve and mobilize African American communities for both community well-being and social justice. Black churches have provided education, banks, and low-income housing; they have also nurtured the artistic talents of musicians and actors and the political aspirations of those who would go on to pursue careers in public service. The connection between Black people and Christian culture is so deep that I am unsure if a sound argument for food justice that fails to mention Christian ethics or values would be impactful.

There is a deep connection between faith and food within the Christian tradition and within Black communities. This connection provides a natural segue where religious belief can and does inform community practice. Christian history shows us that many of Jesus's miracles involved food, and one of the Christian sacraments consists of Jesus's sharing himself with his disciples through food (bread and wine). Furthermore, Christians who pray before meals are generally understood to be acknowledging that the food they are about to consume is a gift from God. Indeed, given the religiosity of the Black community and the importance of Black "soul" in the 1960s, we shouldn't be surprised that the popular expression for Black foodways has become known as *soul* food.

While African American communities are generally religious, the expression of African American religiosity varies along denominational, regional, and theological lines. The theoethical arguments put forth in this book emerge from within the liberationist tradition, which is, in all fairness, a minority tradition within the broader spectrum of African American Christian practice. For those familiar with liberation theologies and ethics, I use the term "antioppressive" as a qualifying adjective to signal my commitment to decolonial methodologies, which I will describe in greater detail below. Theologically I will argue that in light of an antioppressive liberatory theological stance, Christians ought to view food justice as central to how we go about *practicing being human* and practicing Christianity in our everyday lives. While the theoethical response to food injustice I develop is written primarily for Black Christians and Black people, my goal was for all Christians, regardless of their racialization, to find this book a helpful resource in combatting structural racism and food injustice.

DECOLONIZING

My approach to exploring Black foodways is inspired by decolonial thinkers such as Frantz Fanon, Sylvia Winter, Aimé Césaire, Aníbal Quijano, and Walter Mignolo, whose work seeks to undo the horrors of coloniality, the dark underbelly of modernity. Coloniality is the mindset and knowledge system that preceded, accompanied, and made possible colonial encounters. The era, so to speak, of coloniality begins in the 1500s with the genocide of Indigenous peoples in the Americas, the enslavement of Africans as chattel, and the development of totalizing self-serving narratives (e.g., salvation, progress, development) by some European Christian men that were used to justify their destruction of other civilizations.[14] All human beings and the entire biotic world suffer within the modernity/coloniality dualistic worldview. Decolonization is the twin process of identifying and dismantling coloniality in all its forms in order to build something new. Decolonization requires seeking out the hidden aspects of the political, economic, and social ideologies that maintained colonialist thinking even after political independence or civil rights have been achieved.[15]

As Audre Lorde reminded us, "The master's tools will never dismantle the master's house," and decolonial thinking seeks to undue, disobey, and delink from coloniality by building a praxis toward another way of thinking, being, doing, and living.[16] In this way, decoloniality seeks to unsettle a fundamental principle of modernity and envision alternative futures where institutions are at the service of life rather than life being at the service of institutions. Reflecting on Audre Lorde's proclamation, philosophers Lewis Gordon and Jane Anna Gordon suggest that "even if it were true that his house cannot be dismantled by his tools, slaves have historically done something more provocative with such tools than attempt to dismantle the Big House. There are those who used those tools, developed additional ones, and built houses of their own on more or less generous soil. It is our view that the proper response is to follow their lead, transcending rather than dismantling Western ideas through building our own houses of thought."[17] In this way, the aim of decolonial thinking is to do more than dismantle the master's house, it is to use the master's tools and our own to create something that gives us life beyond the restrictions of coloniality. Soul food can and should be used to that end.

My decolonial analysis of Black foodways unfolds in four movements: knowing, thinking, being, and doing, or epistemology, social analysis, theological anthropology, and praxis. Each movement is expounded upon in the following four chapters. Soul food, while not explicitly a decolonial project, easily fits within decolonial praxis, given that it is a way of eating that seeks to subvert and upend Western culinary practices by being explicitly tied to Black culture. The knowledge that produced soul food did not emerge from Eurocentric culture but from the minds of enslaved Africans and their descendants; thus, by its very nature, soul food already seeks to decenter whiteness and white supremacy. Decolonizing soul food, however, also requires it to be delinked from coloniality, the structures and ideologies that support and sustain the hegemonic power of the West.

Delinking presupposes relinking to something else. In this way, decoloniality is both an undoing and redoing, theory and praxis woven together. With respect to Black foodways, I suggest that black veganism (among other practices that I will expand upon as this book unfolds) is the ideal form of soulfull eating and the way Black people can decolonize our diets and delink from coloniality for three reasons.[18] First, black veganism investigates the root and scope of colonial thought by making explicit the connection between the logic of racism and the colonial use of the term "animal." Second, it forces us to explore how white supremacist race-thinking extends beyond Black bodies and is inclusive of nonhuman animals and the biotic community. Third, it forces us to examine how the language of animality and "animal characteristics" has been a tool used to justify the oppression of any being who deviates, by species, race, or behavior, from Western Christian anthropological norms, where the white heterosexual male is considered the ideal godlike being. Black veganism then becomes an ideal way for Black people to eat in a way that prioritizes justice for and solidarity with Black and other dispossessed communities.

Within the framework of Christian theology and ethics, black veganism also helps Christians delink from colonial Christian theological norms that undermine the human dignity of people of color and justify the exploitation of nonhuman animals and the earth. In this way, *black veganism should be viewed as compassionate action that helps us relink to the antioppressive and liberative religion of Jesus.* As Howard Thurman notes in *Jesus and the Disinherited*, the religion of Jesus is often at odds with the ways Christianity is practiced today: "The basic fact is that Christianity as it was born in the mind of this Jewish teacher and thinker appears as a technique of survival for the oppressed. That it became, through the intervening years, a religion of the powerful and dominant, used sometimes as an instrument of oppression, must not tempt us into believing that it was thus in the mind and life of Jesus."[19] Following Thurman, I suggest that the "religion of Jesus" is best understood as a spiritual path of radical compassion. This spiritual path has three dimensions: "a deepening of our connection to the compassion of God, a restoration to a humanity fully loved and alive, and an increase to our capacity to be instruments of compassion toward others in the world."[20] When we consider that Jesus was a Jewish teacher living under Roman colonial occupation, we should not be surprised that these three dimensions are also consistent with decolonial thinking in that they are a profoundly relational way of being in the world that prioritizes defining one's spirituality and self-identity outside of the colonial worldview.

From a social justice perspective, Jesus's spiritual path was rooted in his third way of being in the world. By third way I mean a way of living that resists the dualistic thinking of fight or flight and instead embraces nonviolent resistance when pursuing social justice.[21] This third way is neither submissive nor passive, as it is sometimes interpreted to mean. Instead, the third way asks you to see yourself as created in the image of God, to recognize that your humanity is not defined by the colonial powers, and that liberation from oppression is a communal rather than an individual enterprise. In delinking from the colonial worldview that normalizes the suffering and exploitation of Black and nonhuman animal bodies, black veganism seeks to opt out of structures that normalize violence and suffering and live into ways of being in the world consistent with Jesus's spiritual path of radical compassion and his way of nonviolent social transformation.

Lastly, I want to note that I use the term "black veganism" rather than "veganism" to signal that black veganism differs from uncritical (i.e., ontologically white) adoptions of a vegan diet. Black culture and the experiences of Black people are the starting point for my construction of a Christian black veganism. My identification as Black influences what my veganism looks like and how I suggest people ought to practice veganism.[22] However, the "blackness" of black veganism should be understood ontologically, meaning one does not have to be Black to practice black veganism. Instead, the "blackness" of black veganism signifies a commitment to an antioppressive way of being in the world that grounds our notions of humanity and animality in ways that influence what we consume.

INTERPRETING

Race is an important interpretive lens for my decolonial analysis of Black foodways. Given that I am arguing that the US food system is racist, it is important to be as clear as possible when using race terminology and making claims that an action or structural system is racist.

Americans tend to have a "commonsense" understanding of what race and racism are, meaning that race is merely someone's skin tone and that racism is prejudice toward someone because of said skin tone. Yet the emergence of the Black Lives Matter movement and the rhetoric surrounding the 2016 election of Donald Trump as president of the United States reveal that there is much that Americans disagree on when it comes to race.

In the simplest terms, race is a way of identifying and classifying human beings. As social beings, we categorize the world to make sense of it. Human classifications can help us discern our friends from our enemies, place ourselves within accepted social hierarchies, and guide us in our interactions with the individuals and groups we encounter.[23] However, the very act of defining racial groups has produced both intended and unintended consequences, as our conceptions of race have shifted, producing new and emerging identities. In this way, race can be understood as an "unstable and decentered" web of social meanings that are continually being transformed through political struggle.[24] Although the commonsense understanding of race invokes biologically based human characteristics, we must remember that the selection of biological features used in classification is always a social and historical process. Despite the imprecise and arbitrary history of racial signification, race is not meaningless; it performs ideological work and has real political consequences.

Sociologists Michael Omi and Howard Winant have examined the history of new and emerging racial identities and categorizations in the United States, and their work is helpful in my analysis of the role race plays in our food system. Race should be understood as a "master category—a fundamental concept that has profoundly shaped and continues to shape, the history, polity, economic structure and culture" of the United States.[25] In this way, we recognize that the onset of transatlantic slavery and the encounter with Native Americans were fundamental to race making and categorizing the people who constituted the modern world. Doing so makes it clear that "race has become the template of both difference and inequality," hence its placement as a master category of social organization.[26]

The process of race making and the social order that is subsequently constructed as a result of race making is racial formation, the "sociohistorical process by which racial identities are created, lived out, transformed, and destroyed." To be racially identified is to be located within a social structure that has historically used race to demarcate cultural boundaries, political rights, and economic opportunities. Borrowing from Omi and Winant, I use the term "racial project" to describe how the ideological and practical links between the social structure of society and one's race operate on a day-to-day basis. Consequently, racial projects should also be understood as an effort to organize and distribute resources (economic, political, cultural) along particular racial lines. Racial projects connect what race means in "particular discursive or ideological practice" and elucidate how both "social structure and everyday experiences" are lived out and racially organized based on that meaning.[27]

Racial projects help us understand and explain how racism is embedded in the structural foundation of the US economy, polity, and ideology. Structural racism includes

1. the institutionalized economic and other social resource inequalities that can be traced along racial lines;
2. the institutionalized political marginalization that can be traced along racial lines; and
3. the institutionalized racial ideologies, with ideology being a set of racialized stereotypes, ideas, beliefs, attitudes, emotions, narratives, and so on, that help normalize and moralize racial discrimination.

This framework helps us understand how the domestic and international food systems are racist racial projects; within both systems, the organization and inequitable distribution of goods and services can be traced along particular racial lines that disproportionately marginalize Black, Indigenous, and other people of color. Race has become the template of both difference and equality within the global food system in ways that have proved to be disadvantageous for many people of color. Within both the domestic and global food systems, economic, political, and ideological tools are used to rationalize and justify inequalities.

Indeed, ideology plays a crucial role in normalizing structural racism. When thinking about the structural dimensions of racism, it is easier to focus on (i.e., easier to quantify) racist economic or political inequalities because the unequal distribution of economic or political power can be measured. While ideology is immeasurable in ways that are analogous to economic or political power, its structural significance is no less critical. Human beings live and make meaning within social structures, and the biases, attitudes, and prejudices that they hold influence how the structures operate. Likewise, the biases, attitudes, and prejudices that are built into social structures such as our food system influence how human beings understand and interpret their world. Thus, addressing the structural racism within our food systems requires an honest look at the cultural ideologies that normalize the evil that is food injustice.

Womanist ethicist Emilie Townes describes the ideologies that are used to produce misery and suffering in ways that inform social structures as the cultural production of evil. Her work is helpful in my analysis of the racial, gendered, and class ideologies of food because she suggests that "to understand structural evil is to recognize, from the outset, that the story can be told in another way."[28] *Ideologies (re)shape memory.* Food justice for Black people, then, requires us to delink the colonial images and narratives from our historical analysis of Black foodways in order to develop the other side of the story, or decolonial countermemories.

The images of Black folks and food and the narratives tied to them have helped shape the memories of all people who have lived in the United States. To be sure, the negative images, stereotypes, and ideologies that surround Black foodways were generated within what Townes calls the "white fantastic hegemonic imagination," which "traffics in people's lives that are caricatured or pillaged so that the imagination that creates the fantastic can control the world in its own image. . . . It is this imagination that helps to hold systemic, structural evil in place." While it is the case that the ideologies that normalize structural evil in ways that harm Black people were created by some white people, most people, regardless of race, have internalized the white fantastic imagination. The white fantastic imagination is a product of coloniality. The decolonial challenge, then, is to develop new ways of being human and renewed knowledges that help us resist developing Black foodways by the ideological stereotypes and denigrating myths of the white fantastic hegemonic imagination.[29]

THE RECIPE FOR THE BOOK

My decolonial analysis of Black foodways unfolds in four movements: knowing, thinking, being, and doing, or epistemology, social analysis, anthropology, and praxis. Each movement is expounded upon in chapters 1 through 4.

Chapter 1, "Transatlantic Soul," provides an examination of the dietary evolution of people of African descent and pays special attention to Black folk in the United States. I examine the history and development of African American foodways by exploring how dietary practices evolved from West Africa to slave plantations and finally to our contemporary kitchens. Using a culinary and linguistic perspective, I pay special attention to the dietary customs that were connected with religious rituals, as well as to the evolution of "soul food." I argue that by fully embracing the legacy that is Black soul, Black Christians leave room for the evolution of our conceptual notions of what constitutes soul food.

In chapter 2, "Food Pyramid Scheme," I provide a modern historical analysis of the political economy of food as it relates to African Americans and the global poor. I explain how our food system has developed in ways that have normalized the racist exploitation of the labor of people of color. I then examine the impact of environmental racism on food policies and the corporate practices that limit access to healthy and fresh food in poor, urban, and mostly Black neighborhoods. I will argue that US food policies are designed to benefit middle- and upper-class Americans, as well as multinational food corporations, at the expense of local developing economies.

Chapter 3, "Being Human as Praxis," provides the theoethical framework for the social justice praxis that I suggest in chapter 4. Within Christianity, the oppression of Black people was justified through theological norms that viewed Black bodies as "Other" and on the anthropological theory that Blacks were less rational and therefore less human than whites. Thus, the theoethical problem confronting many African American Christians has been our unknowing adoption of a racist and sexist theological anthropology that justifies the exploitation of nature, humans, and nonhuman animals. Indeed, this theological anthropology has led some of us to, at times, justify racial disparities (both domestic and global) as a product of "culture" when in fact racial discrimination is the sole cause of such disparities. Using the work of feminist, liberationist, womanist, and biblical scholars, I end this chapter by beginning to fashion a liberative antioppressive theological anthropology that creates an alternative vision of what the God-human encounter entails for Christians and clarifies the role we should play in the pursuit of food and environmental justice.

Chapter 4, "Tasting Freedom," is constructive in nature and attempts to answer the question I asked at the beginning of the book: What should soul food look like today? More specifically, I develop theologically informed eating practices for African American Christians that are socially and politically liberative. I propose that African American Christians should adopt three theologically grounded eating practices in response to food injustice.

The first and most important practice, *soulfull eating*, builds upon my definition of soul to explain how soul food can still honor the past while forging a new, socially critical, and healthier future. I suggest that to eat soulfully is to practice an *agent-specific and context-specific* black veganism. To be sure, veganism is often associated with white people who have too much disposable income and only care about animal suffering. This type of noncritical veganism does exist. However, black veganism as I define it is to eat in a way that decenters whiteness, challenges capitalism and colonialism, and reclaims the Black culinary and ecological heritage. The second practice is *seeking justice for food workers*, which discusses the ramifications of justice for agricultural workers, as well as arguments for how we should purchase and grow our own food and move toward creating food-sovereign spaces. The third practice is *caring for the earth,* and I will argue that earth care as it relates to food justice is a distinct and vital part of Christian practice.

Each chapter ends with a vegan soul-full recipe that is intended to help us weave together the complicated tapestry that is Black faith, Black foodways, and Black culture. I include these recipes for two reasons. First, you may think that in adopting black veganism you will have to give up eating certain foods that are so steeped in the Black culinary canon that you cannot imagine not eating them. These recipes are my attempt to demonstrate that while there are some things I am asking you to give up, taste, flavor, and traditional soul food dishes are not among them. Second, my transition from vegetarianism to veganism took place over an eight-year period, and the ideological transition (i.e., feelings and identity surrounding certain foods) was much more complicated than the practical transition (i.e., creating vegan versions of soul food dishes). These recipes tell the story of that transition. I had to experiment in order to figure out how to cook food that *felt and tasted* like "home." These recipes are the fruits of that labor. I have identified certain brand-name products that I like, but I am by no means a chef, so you should substitute items as necessary to suit you or your family's tastes! Be creative and experiment with these recipes as you move along your own culinary journey.

RED BEANS AND RICE

For me, a Black man whose American ancestry begins in Mississippi and Louisiana, the foundational soul food dish will always be red beans and rice. This recipe was a staple in my childhood, something we could eat on special occasions and when our budget for food was slim. For me, *red beans and rice feels like home.* When the pervasive reality of racism knocks me off-center, red beans and rice can be the ground from which I can regain my sense of self and remember myself as beloved by my community and beloved by the Ultimate source of compassion. Despite all the stress and the micro- and macroaggressions I may face, sitting down at the dinner table and eating red beans give me a little something to help me keep on keeping on, as the elders would say.

If we think about the history of Black foodways as a window into the racism that was and continues to be foundational to our domestic food system, we realize that Black foodways have a deeper meaning that can easily be overlooked. Knowing this history and finding ourselves within this story prompt theological reflection and response. Decolonial analysis seeks to unsettle the notion that theory and praxis are necessarily separate from each other—theory is thinking, and thinking is doing, and praxis necessarily requires thought-reflection on actions. Both my Christian faith and my identity as a Black man influence the analysis, arguments, and constructive proposals that I put forth in this book. What some might see as a provocative suggestion, black veganism, is rooted in these two identities. However, what follows in this book is not a straightforward argument for veganism. My own path to veganism was not straightforward. It was a complicated and challenging transition, and it would be foolish to expect otherwise from anyone, especially from Black people, given the ways that our foodways are racialized.

Black veganism is a process of being and becoming, knowing who we are and what tools we need to use so that Black foodways can be a source of abundant life for Black communities.

When I became vegetarian and subsequently transitioned to veganism, I feared that my evolving diet compromised my ability to feel like I was a part of my community when we sat down for meals. Moreover, if I could not eat red beans and rice, I wondered what kind of Black person I would be. Could I still claim to be standing on the culinary shoulders of my ancestors? Finding a vegan version of this dietary staple opened my eyes to the creativity one can have cooking soul food. Preparing it and serving it to my family revealed that this delicious version conjures the same familial memories as its nonhuman animal meat–based alternative; thus, it possesses the strength to become a foundational family dish too. Because of this, red beans and rice is the first dish we set out upon our vegan soul food table.[30] This recipe serves six people.

Ingredients

1 tablespoon grapeseed oil (or any high-heat oil)

1 large white onion, diced medium

6 6-inch celery stalks, diced small

6 garlic cloves, minced

4 vegan sausages (I highly recommend Field Roast Vegetarian Grain Meat Sausages, either Smoked Apple Sage, Italian, or Mexican Chipotle flavor)

1 teaspoon chili powder

1 teaspoon Cajun seasoning

1 teaspoon dried thyme

4 cups of broth made from Better Than Bouillon Seasoned Vegetable Base

2 15-ounce cans of kidney beans, rinsed and drained

1 red bell pepper, cored, seeded, and chopped

2 cups cooked basmati rice

½ cup green onions

Directions

Heat a 4- or 5-quart stew pot over high heat, add the oil, and wait until it shimmers. Add the onion and celery and cook, stirring with a wooden spoon, until translucent, about 10 minutes. Add the garlic and cook about 2 minutes more. Add the sausage, chili powder, Cajun seasoning, thyme, broth, beans, and bell pepper. Bring to a simmer and cook for 10–15 minutes, stirring frequently. Season with salt, pepper, and your favorite hot sauce. Serve over a bed of rice, and garnish with the green onions.

Chapter 1
Transatlantic Soul

A heaping helping of fried chicken, macaroni and
cheese, collard greens too big for my jeans. Smoke
steams from under the lid that's on the pot, ain't never
had a lot but thankful for the little that I got. Why that
be, fast food got me feeling sick, them crackers think
they slick by trying to make this bullshit affordable. I
thank the Lord that my voice was recordable. . . . Come
and get yo' soul food, well well. Good old-fashioned
soul food, all right. Everything is for free, as good as it
can be. Come and get some soul food.
—Goodie Mob, "Soul Food"

Goodie Mob was a hip-hop group whose members hailed from the
southern United States, and "Soul Food" is the title track from their
critically acclaimed debut album, which appeared in November 1995.
The song waxes poetic about the foods they love to eat—foods they
believe are good for the soul. At the same time, the song and the music
video criticize the fast food industry for targeting Black communities
by selling food they believe to be harmful to our health and well-being.
Most poignantly, they argue that eating "good old-fashioned soul food"
is a community event, a time when people feed those who may not be
able to feed themselves just because they are a part of "our" community.

"Soul Food" melodically articulates a spiritual truth held by many
African Americans, the idea that since our ancestors found strength
in eating a particular diet, we not only pay homage to them by eating
similarly but also find strength. However, how did we come to "know"

what our ancestors ate? When does our ancestral culinary history begin, and when did it end, or, rather, has it ended?

My quest to answer these questions brought me to the old plantations in southern Louisiana. Several states have their own "river roads" where you can visit old plantations, but none is as well-known as Louisiana's. Louisiana's fabled Mississippi River Road consists of a corridor approximately seventy miles in length located on each side of the river between Baton Rouge and New Orleans. The area includes the river, levees, and adjacent lands and cultural resources. Among the latter is the state's most famous and recognizable group of monumental plantation houses, most built by wealthy sugar planters in the Greek Revival style (figure 1).

My goal in visiting and researching these plantations was to learn as much as I could about the agricultural skills the enslaved Africans brought with them that would ultimately be exploited by their owners. I wish I could say that each plantation I visited was able to share information about the enslaved Africans and their owners. I wish I could say that each tour guide knew more about the agriculture of the planta-

Figure 1. The "big house" on Whitney Plantation. Photo taken in June 2016 by the author.

tions than I learned through my own research prior to visiting. I wish these things because it should be improbable to work on a former slave plantation and to make the same mistakes that the white enslavers who owned the plantation made—to dehumanize and render invisible the Black people who were forced to live, work, and die on that property.

The Whitney Plantation was the only plantation that told the story of the property in ways that humanized and gave voice to the enslaved. Walking the grounds with Dr. Ibrahima Seck, a Senegalese historian who has written about the Whitney Plantation, added depth and complexity to the story of African enslavement.[1] "We are an agricultural people," he said over and over during our walk. Seck suggests that among the reasons why African enslavement was successful was that slavers knew what ethnic group of Africans to purchase based upon where they were going to sell them. Moreover, because these microcommunities of African ethnic groups existed on many plantations, African foodways and agricultural practices were able to survive.

Decolonizing soul food begins by delinking it from agricultural and dietary practices that uphold the logics of coloniality. The purpose of this chapter, then, is to unearth some of the dietary and agricultural practices among enslaved Africans to lay the epistemological foundation for the development of new liberatory and antioppressive foodways. To do so, I explore the history and development of African American eating by surveying how dietary practices evolved from West Africa to slave plantations to our contemporary kitchens. I pay special attention to the gendered ideologies that evolved around Black foodways, particularly the ideologies that sustain current notions of what constitutes soul food. How might a reevaluation of what we think we know about gender, agriculture, and Black foodways help us envision something new? What role can compassion play in helping attend to the trauma that lingers within so many Black people with respect to agriculture and Black foodways?

DECOLONIZING KNOWLEDGE

Social analysis is neither objective nor capable of being completely neutral. Consequently, my analysis of the agricultural and culinary history of African and African American people privileges the knowledge compiled by members of those communities. The challenge of this task is thus to distinguish between colonial knowledge that has been pressed upon Black communities through coloniality and decolonizing knowledges that continue to reconnect Black people to our truest sense of who we are.

To break free from social, political, and ideological structures that inhibit freedom, African Americans and all marginalized peoples should critically examine what we have come to call "knowledge" so that we are able to recognize that there are different ways of knowing beyond what we may have learned within our current culture. That is, we must examine our epistemological assumptions. The dominant ways of knowing within the United States evolved from Western philosophical and theological traditions. As Latin American ecofeminist liberation theologian Ivone Gebara has argued, these traditions have always had an anthropocentric and androcentric bias, and within the United States these theories of knowing also have a Eurocentric or white bias. The knowledge that people of color, women, and the poor have is often referred to as "experiential knowledge, knowledge based on everyday experience" by Eurocentric culture; however, knowledge of this sort "[is] not automatically recognized as real knowing."[2] While this does not mean that Eurocentric ways of knowing are necessarily *wrong*, it does mean that they are *limited*. By not including people of color and women in the construction of so-called legitimate knowledge, the knowledge fostered by dominant white culture has lost and continues to lose vital contributions to its construction.

Liberation begins through learning and unlearning knowledges that undo the normative grip of coloniality on our consciousness. Decolonizing our knowing is a liberative act because our knowing informs our thinking and shapes our being—what we know about ourselves informs the stories we tell ourselves, and those stories help shape who we see ourselves being and becoming. On a practical level, epistemology informs and shapes ontology. In this way, liberation is more than just a culminating moment in the future. Liberation is a decolonial process, a process of letting go of the narratives that kept us tied to coloniality by grounding ourselves in the truth of who we are and whom we aim to be, a process of decolonizing our knowledge and placing institutions at the service of life, a process of thinking and imagining social systems that sustain and promote life.[3]

The knowledge hierarchy within the dominant culture of the United States parallels the race, class, and gender hierarchies of modern society. These hierarchies sustain the economic, political, and ideological logic of oppression by excluding the knowledge of the marginalized for the sake of preserving the current power structure, which privileges only the smallest percentage of society. This hierarchy of knowledge is so accepted in our culture that it often goes unquestioned. For Black people, women, and the poor, "the history of domination has so deeply marked the foundations of our culture that [the oppressed] end up claiming, as if it were our own, the type of knowledge put out by those who hold political and economic power."[4] As such, decolonizing epistemology is a critical step in our analysis of Black foodways so that we can identify the barriers that have been put in place to hinder our ability to know and accept knowledge crafted outside of the spheres of coloniality as legitimate knowledge. Decolonial knowing becomes constitutive of the process that interrogates these hierarchies of knowledge and the ideological assumptions that normalize racism, sexism, classism, and food injustice.

As it relates to African American culinary and agricultural knowledge, decolonizing our knowing begins by exploring the history of West African agriculture and foodways in order to discern what knowledges enslaved Africans brought with them to colonial America. Ecowomanist and social ethicist Melanie Harris helpfully describes this process as "mining ecomemory," exploring and honoring the collective ecological experiences of Black people in general and specifically Black women. Ecomemories can be "a collective set of values that guide the earth commitments of an entire community or a singular story that reflects the themes or values about the environment and one's connection to the earth."[5] By recalling and retelling these ecomemories, we are able to expose hidden or forgotten truths and debunk the myths and stereotypes that permeate Black agricultural and culinary history.[6] In this way, ecomemories can serve as decolonial countermemories that seek to reconstitute a colonial ecological history that often ignores or stereotypes nonwhite bodies and claims Black agricultural and culinary ingenuity as its own. This quest asks us to explore how African diasporic agricultural and culinary knowledges have evolved during the last five hundred years. What knowledges must be gained and retained, and what must we let go of if we are to delink our foodways from coloniality and relink them into a just and sustainable food system? Knowing in this critical self-reflective way is the first step in the cultivation of an antioppressive consciousness.

FROM AFRICA TO AMERICA: AGRICULTURAL AND CULINARY HISTORY

The fact that African agricultural and animal husbandry knowledge was critical to the growth of New World plantations is rarely, if ever, mentioned when the story of African enslavement is being told. This convenient omission breathes life into the myth and assumption that enslaved Africans had no legitimate knowledge except for what they were taught by their white enslavers.

Geographers Judith Carney and Richard Rosomoff suggest that Africans began the process of domesticating plant and animal species around 10,500 BP in the areas surrounding the present-day Sahara Desert. The agricultural skillset they honed over the next eight thousand years made them particularly valuable to white slavers, as African knowledge proved vital on plantations and ranches in the United States. Within West and sub-Saharan Africa, cattle domestication evolved to include a variety of species to offset the threat of drought, given that each species "grazed in different parts of the grasslands or consumed plants unpalatable to the others." African herders experimented with cross-breeding cattle to develop breeds that were more suited to their specific climate, and this knowledge was passed down through generations. When we compare the ranching practices of colonial America to that of preslavery West Africa, it is clear that "livestock-raising peoples such as the Fula brought animal husbandry skills that contributed critically to the New World ranching traditions." Regarding plant domestication, Africans eventually developed agricultural techniques such as multicropping and intercropping systems that included the "cultivation of seed plants, tubers, and legumes with valuable fruit, nut, and oil-bearing trees."[7] This agricultural method reduced soil erosion from tropical downpours and created a natural deterrent to prevent insects from ruining their crops, again, methods that New World plantation owners would replicate. African farmers and herdsmen both adapted to and altered their surroundings to provide for their communities. Similarly, within the history of African and African American foodways, adaptation and improvisation became vital principles.

Food historian Jessica Harris has written extensively on the development of African American foodways. She argues that the earliest records of what would become African American culinary habits can be seen in the travels of Abdallah Ibn Battuta, "a famous Tangine traveler, [who] left Marrakesh in 1352 to head for Bilad al Sudan (the place of the blacks)." Ibn Battuta was sent by the sultan of Morocco to the kingdom of Mali to learn more about the culture and the people, some of whom were Morocco's primary trading partners. Ibn Battuta wrote detailed accounts of the food and agricultural practices of the people he encountered in addition to his primary task of encouraging continued trade. During his two-year journey, he crossed the Sahara, visited salt mines, encountered gardens filled with truffles, and tasted a variety of foods. Ibn Battuta's account is particularly useful for the reconstruction of African American foodways because he traveled to the regions that would ultimately dominate the slave trade. His writings reveal that many elements of African American foodways are reflected in the patterns of African eating he witnessed almost seven hundred years ago. These elements include various cooking techniques commonly used by slaves and African Americans today, a women-driven marketplace that mirrors the primary role played by African American women in agriculture and the selling of food, a tradition of warm hospitality, and the ritual importance of food.[8]

Food was indeed an essential part of ritual in West Africa. Harris finds that there are generally two basic types of traditional holidays: the first offers thanksgiving and sacrifice to the ancestors and the gods, while the second celebrates the new harvest. Examples of religious rituals involving food were evident in the region of modern-day Senegal, where inhabitants poured milk into the sea to placate Mame Coumba

Castel, the spirit of the island, and "symbolically fed" mashed yams "to the sacred stools of Ashanti." Another example can be seen in the regions of modern-day Ghana and Nigeria, where the traditional yam festival, Homowowo, which commemorates the communities' triumph over hunger and famine, is still celebrated today. In Ghana, Nigeria, and other West African countries where yam was a primary starch, yam celebrations "range from new yam shoots being paraded" through a community to ensure a prosperous harvest to an "elder or community leader reading yam peels" as a way to predict the crop yield for the upcoming season. Having both studied and experienced modern-day versions of these festivals, Harris argues that many of the culinary rituals of Africa resonate in ways similar to African American religious and cultural rituals, where food is also an integral aspect of thanksgiving, celebration, and worship.[9]

While Ibn Battuta's journey predates Columbus's journey across the Atlantic by almost 150 years, one cannot minimize the influence of Columbus and other colonialists from Portugal, Spain, and Britain on African foodways. The African continent became an essential part of the triangular trade between the American colonies and Britain. European colonialists brought foods such as corn, tomatoes, chilies, and cassava from North and South America to Africa. In her several journeys to West Africa, Harris observed that many of the aforementioned foods from the Americas have become "so emblematic of [West Africa's] cuisine that it is almost impossible to imagine its dishes without them." These vegetables became a part of the continent's traditional dishes, which tend to be soupy stews poured over either a starch or grilled animal protein and often accompanied by a vegetable sauce and starch.[10]

Due to climate differences, only a small number of foods that could adapt to the new environment were brought from the African continent to the United States. However, three of the few plants that did survive are emblematic of African American cookery today: okra, watermelon, and black-eyed peas. Okra most likely made its way to colonial America via the Caribbean and has had a long-standing relationship with Black and southern cooking. It is highly valued in Africa as a "thickener," and the slippery mucilage it exudes makes it a great base

ingredient for several soupy stews.[11] Watermelon has such a complicated history with African Americans that we should not be surprised
to learn that the fruit is believed to have originated on the continent
of Africa. Paintings of watermelons can be found in Egyptian tombs,
and in southern Africa watermelons have been eaten for centuries.[12]
Similar to watermelon, black-eyed peas can be traced to Egyptian tombs
as well. In the Americas, Black people most commonly associate the
bean with New Year's Day, when many present-day African Americans
and southerners eat hoppin' John, a bean and rice dish, ostensibly to
bring good fortune into the new year.

Most of the African slaves who would become the ancestors to
present-day African Americans were transplanted from the western
coasts of Africa, where the agricultural practices of the various king-
doms revolved around three crops: corn, rice, and yams. The wide
band below the Sahara, from present-day Sudan in the east to Senegal
in the west, cultivated sorghum and several varieties of millet. The
coastal area in the Niger Delta region, which includes the remaining
portions of present-day Senegal and the Republic of Guinea, cultivated rice. The third area, which includes the Ivory Coast and Cam-
eroon, cultivated yams. The agricultural practices of these particular
Africans were crucial because the herding and agricultural skillsets
they brought with them from their homelands helped determine
where they could be sold for the highest price. These agricultural
skills would prove to be life-saving. Once the enslaved Africans arrived
in the colonies, they would be responsible for feeding not only their
owners' pockets but also their owners' families and, in many cases,
their own.

THE AFRICAN HAND STIRRED THE FOOD OF COLONIAL AMERICA

The connection between food and enslavement extends beyond the
mere consumption of certain foods to include the agricultural cycles of
West African nations. Historian Stephen Behrendt makes a compelling
argument that the supply and demand of African slaves were linked
to the seasonal production of three West African staple foods (corn,
rice, yams) and American cash crops.[13] African slave traders would

purchase slaves from farming communities, and along with the slaves, traders would purchase the requisite foods that were needed to keep the slaves alive during the Middle Passage.

The Africans who were brought to colonial America endured a hellish journey. Much ink has been used to describe the horrific conditions of the slave ships, yet it was within these ships that Africans began to shape the culinary tastes of colonial America. Slave ships would have required more food than any other ships traveling the Atlantic because the cargo itself needed to eat. The captains and those who invested in slave ships had an economic interest in keeping the slaves alive and feeding them something that would help them look fit enough to sell once they reached their destinations. As a result, the three staple foods were taken aboard the ship because they represented the three food regions of West Africa.

Given the importance placed upon food, the cook was a critical part of the ship's crew, and cooking was no easy task. Cooks would spend most of their days in the galleys of ships, preparing meals for anywhere between three hundred and four hundred slaves and thirty or so crew members. By the eighteenth century, the role of the cook became increasingly assigned to Africans, either enslaved or free. These African cooks were responsible for creating foodstuffs that the slaves and crew alike would eat. Given that many slaves would attempt to starve themselves, choosing to die rather than face the unknown that lay ahead, being a cook was a dangerous occupation, because cooks were liable to be blamed when slaves did not eat. However, because slaves often possessed the linguistic capability to communicate with other Africans, even if they were from another area of Africa, cooks would often find ways to encourage the slaves to eat. During these long voyages, women also helped with food preparation and were assigned tasks such as milling corn and husking rice.[14] In this way, the African hand began shaping the tastes of colonial America even before the slave ships docked.

Upon arrival to colonial America, the African palate continued to influence colonial food by stirring and seasoning the food prepared in colonial kitchens (figure 2). Slaves who were chosen to work in the "big house" were tasked with its care and maintenance, as well as the

Figure 2. This picture, taken at the Whitney Plantation in Louisiana, shows the kitchen and its proximity to the master's house. Photo taken in June 2016 by the author.

care and maintenance of its inhabitants. Working in the big house has a complicated history within Black culture, given that some regard house servants as the elite class of slavery.[15] However, the idea of an "elite class" of slaves is built upon the false notion that these slaves had some degree of special privilege that allowed them to avoid the labor of the fields, which was perceived as being more difficult. However, often overlooked is the fact that these slaves had to live at the beck and call of their masters, which often required them to sleep on the floor outside the bedroom in case the master needed anything during the night. Moreover, their chores revolved around meeting every need of their masters. From breakfast preparation to the evening turndown, the house slaves were working. The lack of privacy, coupled with the requirement to work without rest and the fear of sexual assault, must have been grueling, a type of suffering entirely different but no less painful from that of fieldwork.

The role of the cook within the big house was vital. Because of the significance placed on food, we ought to view the big house kitchen as a space of power during the antebellum period in the South. The cook, whether on his or her own or in conjunction with the mistress of the house, oversaw the entire feeding operation. Depending on the size of the plantation, the cook could be responsible for feeding not only his or her master's family but also all the workers on the plantation. If the master was one of the wealthier plantation owners, his dinner gatherings could include twenty or more guests almost every evening. The ideological construction of Black identity during this period of American history suggested that Blacks were not only fit for and excellent at hard labor but also born to cook. Harris quotes Louisianan Charles Gayarré's elaboration on the prevailing sentiment held by white people during the nineteenth century in an article written for an 1880 issue of *Harper's Magazine*: "The Negro is a born cook. He could neither read nor write, and therefore he could not learn from books. He was simply inspired; the god of the spit and the saucepan had breathed into him; that was enough."[16]

Throughout the early history of the United States, the hands that turned the spits of hearth ovens and served beer and ale to the founding fathers were also Black and, surprisingly to modern sensibilities, male.[17] In fact, due to the risk of fire, hearth cooking was so dangerous that for safety reasons the kitchens were often not connected to the main house (figure 2). Initially, most of the cooks were men, because the white enslavers believed that men could survive the dangerous conditions of the hearth somewhat better than women. Two of America's most celebrated patriots, George Washington and Thomas Jefferson, enjoyed the culinary talents of Black male cooks, Hercules and James Hemings.

Little is known about Hercules, but historians presume that he honed his culinary skills at George Washington's home at Mount Vernon, where he was named chief cook in 1786. When the nation's capital was New York City, George Washington had Hercules brought from Virginia to take over as his master chef after becoming dissatisfied with his previous cook. When the capital moved to Philadelphia, Hercules moved there as well. Martha Washington's grandson was quoted as describing Hercules as "highly accomplished and as proficient in the culinary art as could be found in the United States." Hercules's responsibilities would have extended beyond merely cooking, for any head chef would have been responsible for the smooth operation of the entire food operation, from finding the perfect fruits and vegetables to serve, to training servers in the appropriate techniques of formal dining. Fortunately for Hercules, he was able to run away and avoid being caught. He did not return to Mount Vernon at the end of Washington's second term in office. Washington spared no expense to find him and wrote in his journal that "the running off of my cook has been a most inconvenient thing to this family."[18]

The story of James Hemings is one of triumph and tragedy. After Thomas Jefferson's appointment as the commerce secretary to France in 1784, nineteen-year-old James (older brother of Sally Hemings) accompanied Jefferson to Paris in order to be trained in the art of French cuisine. He apprenticed under a French caterer and pastry chef during his first few years in Paris. However, "his most important training was under the chef of the Prince de Condé, in the kitchen at Chateau Chantilly. Chateau Chantilly was today's equivalent of a Michelin five-star kitchen; its cooking considered superior to the food at Versailles." By 1787 Hemings was the head chef at Hôtel de Langeac, which was Jefferson's private residence and America's first diplomatic embassy. Having learned to speak French, Hemings supervised a large French cooking staff and cooked for presidents and royalty. Hemings's style and recipes greatly influenced Virginia plantation cooking and fine food preparation, which spread to the mid-Atlantic region and were adopted in kitchens north and south.[19]

James Hemings should have been a household name to every American who desired to become a chef. Although he bought his freedom in 1796, the challenge of finding work as a Black chef and not merely a Black cook drove him into a depression, and he committed suicide in 1801. James Hemings was the first American to be trained as a French chef. He introduced crème brulée, meringues and French-style whipped cream, European-style macaroni and cheese, ice cream, and french fries to America. His culinary imprint permeates southern fine dining. He is an example of Black culinary genius: entrepreneurial, multilingual, and determined to be treated as an equal. And for this reason, the stories of James Hemings, Hercules, and others like them were hidden because they did not fit the ideologies that white America desired to craft of Black people.

FOOD, GENDER, RACE, AND THE WHITE IMAGINATION

As already noted, ideology plays an important role in normalizing the everydayness of structural racism. The cultural ideologies of Black foodways and the narratives tied to those images have helped shape the memories of many people who have lived in the United States. Specifically, the negative images, stereotypes, and assumptions that surround Black foodways were generated within a white fantastic hegemonic imagination that has helped hold a structurally evil food system in place. As previously noted, in an effort to help rationalize African enslavement, the ideologies surrounding Black cookery and agricultural acumen before emancipation were mostly positive. Black men and women were believed to possess spiritual gifts that enabled them to be excellent farmers and domestic cooks. However, the end of the Civil War brought about a shift in the white imagination's ideological construction of Black culinary skills in an effort to maintain a structurally racist system where whites would benefit at the expense of Black people.

In her book *Building Houses out of Chicken Legs: Black Women, Food, and Power,* American studies scholar and food historian Psyche Williams-Forson argues that white society in the post–Civil War era felt the need to put free Blacks in their place, and the primary means used to accomplish that was the subjugation and humiliation of Black men. It was during this era that the image of the Zip Coon became popular, since it mocked Black men who had any aspirations—economic, political, social, or cultural.[20]

Figure 3. "A Hot Old Time in Coon Town." Poster advertisement for a minstrel show. Library of Congress.

Zip Coons (figure 3) were purportedly Black men more focused on style than substance. They dressed flashily (i.e., they wore shiny shoes, derbies, and brightly colored vests or blazers) to give the appearance of privilege and equality with white society. However, as the written description on figure 3 conveys, Zip Coons purportedly lacked the intellect to focus on anything other than having a "good old time" and satisfying their worldly desires; in the case of food, their desires for chicken and watermelon were insatiable.

The complex picture of Black men and chicken can be illustrated in the life of Roy Hawkins, a Black man who was the headwaiter at the Coon Chicken Inn in Salt Lake City, Utah (figures 4 and 5). The menu for the restaurant is the face of a Black male Zip Coon; even more shocking is the fact that patrons had to walk through the mouth of the Black male Coon to enter the restaurant. There is no documentation that explains why Maxon Graham, the founder of the Coon Chicken Inn, chose the logo. However, during an interview with Williams-Forson, Hawkins "offered that the logo was a favorite for children and a big draw for families."[21] When we consider the logo in light of the ideological construction of Black men, the Coon Chicken Inn seem-

Figure 4. Coon Chicken Inn menu. Jim Crow Museum of Racist Memorabilia.

Figure 5. Coon Chicken Inn restaurant. Jim Crow Museum of Racist Memorabilia.

ingly projected the idea that they served the best chicken because Black men knew how to find and cook the best chicken.

Black men were caricatured throughout the restaurant—from the menu, which depicted smiling Zip Coons happily serving chicken, to the toothpicks, which were shaped in the faces of smiling Zip Coons. To be sure, Hawkins understood the legacy of the word "coon" as a racial slur referring to Black people, and while working at the Coon Chicken Inn he dealt with the stresses of racial aggression daily. However, Hawkins, like countless other Black men and women, chose to work and provide for his family as his primary form of resistance, despite the difficulties he often faced as a result.

Beyond the characterization of Zip Coon, there also existed a hypersexualization of Black men as "studs," one fueled by white men's fears that Blacks were a threat to white men's virility and to white women's bodies. It is no wonder, then, that Zip Coons were often pictured chasing chicken (i.e., white meat as a euphemism for white women) or engaging in cockfighting. These images were used to single out Black men because "their cocks (literally and figuratively) were often perceived as bigger and better. In this instance, the cock is an object that potentially

Figure 6. Postcard, n.d. Jim Crow Museum of Racist Memorabilia.

symbolizes both the sexual prowess and the confidence of some Black men."[22] The stereotype of the Black male sexual predator is rooted in the misconception that all Black men have enlarged penises and excessive confidence, given their newly found freedom. Images such as the one shown in figure 6 of the "primitive brute" Black male preparing to "consume" a white woman for breakfast played a significant role in perpetuating the ideology that Black men needed to be controlled and therefore symbolically justified the economic and social mistreatment, jailing, and ultimately lynching of countless Black people.

Perhaps the most successful ideological tool used to fuel prejudiced attitudes toward Black men after the Reconstruction era was D. W. Griffith's *Birth of a Nation*, a cinematic adaptation of Thomas Dixon's novel *The Clansman: An Historical Romance of the Ku Klux Klan*. Initially titled *The Clansman* for the first month of its release, *The Birth of a Nation* was the first feature-length movie produced in the United States, with an approximate running time of three hours.[23] Despite its length, it was an immediate success, with over two hundred million people viewing the film in theaters between 1915 and 1946.[24] The popularity and long-running success of the movie cause us to take seriously the influence its caricature of Black male behavior likely had on perpetuating racist ideological stereotypes.

The film portrays the post–Civil War Reconstruction era as a time when "barbaric hordes of lustful and ignorant Blacks," who were given positions of political power by northern white politicians who wanted to profit from the ruins of the South financially, shattered the South's "*natural*" aristocracy.[25] The movie primarily paints a picture of Black men (white men in blackface) in leadership positions as Zip Coons lusting for both political power and power over white women's bodies—powers and privileges that are supposedly reserved for white men. In the climax of the film, Elsie, a virtuous southern woman, is rescued from having to marry a Black man by southern Klansmen, who rise up and restore the natural southern order to American life.[26]

In a society built upon anti-Black racism, the importance of ideology in maintaining structural racism becomes apparent when analyzing *The Birth of a Nation* and the figures included here. The fantastic white imagination seeks to create a worldview through these mythological ideologies, which declare them as factual history. Once accepted as history, the images and the ideologies that reinforce them help shape economic policies (i.e., Black people are poor because they are lazy Zip Coons!) and political policies (i.e., Black people shouldn't have political power, because look what happened during Reconstruction when they had political power!) in ways that normalize structural racism. In other words, ideological manipulation becomes the linchpin in the psyche of some white people that allows—or, even worse, justifies and demands—the existence of oppressive economic and social arrangements because "common sense" deems them necessary.

While Black men may have been perceived as important targets for the justification of Black oppression, Black women endured much of the same treatment. Just like that of their male counterparts, the ideological construction of Black women and food has shifted over time. During slavery, as hearth ovens became less dangerous and less prone to cause house fires, Black women became the primary cooks on slave plantations. As previously described, meal preparation was an arduous task, and these cooks likely embodied discipline and required it of anyone tasked with working under their supervision. Indeed, white people praised other white people for the culinary expertise of their Black female cooks. While referencing pre–Civil War plantation life, Robert Q. Mallard, Presbyterian minister and editor of the *Southwestern Presbyterian Magazine*, once quipped: "French cooks are completely outdistanced in the production of wholesome, dainty and appetizing food; for if, there is any one thing for which the African female intellect has natural genius, it is for cooking."[27] In this way, pre–Civil War stereotypes suggested that Black women possessed a particular patience, discipline, and fortitude that enabled them to create culinary magic in the kitchen.

However, the end of slavery brought about a shift in the form of the stereotype that the dominant society used to describe Black women's culinary skills. No longer was it a sign of strength, discipline, and patience. To keep Black women in their designated "place," their skills became reflected in mammy imagery. In this way, European American culture projected images of Black women cooking and serving white people as the hallmark of their accomplishment and as among the most important work they would ever be capable of doing. The images also typically portrayed Black women as desexualized or

Figure 7. Black Mammy cooking for white family, *Associated Newspapers*, 1921.

"Girls, we will be well fed here; we are fortunate. I have just seen the cook: not a mere black woman that does the cooking, but one bearing a patent stamped by the broad seal of Nature; the type of a class whose skill is not of books or training, but a gift both rich and rare; who flourishes her spit as Amphitrite does

Figure 8. Black cook from *Harper's Weekly*, ca. 1856. Library of Congress.

exoticized, heavyset, and adorned with a headscarf and large white apron (figures 7 and 8).

These nineteenth- and early twentieth-century images attempt to reinforce various stereotypes of Black women. If you look at the image of the mammified Black woman cooking an apple tart for the white children (figure 7), her sole interest in cooking is to please her employer and his children. With her wry smile and the smiling children, the image sends the message that for Black women cooking for white families is among the keys to happiness and economic stability. Indeed, a white person reading the caption of this image would likely surmise that given the mammy's broken English and happy smile, what else could she be qualified to do, and what else would she possibly want to do?

The caption above the image of the woman cooking turkey (figure 8), which appeared in *Harper's Weekly Magazine* before the Civil War, reads in part: "Girls, we will be well fed here; we are fortunate. I have just seen the cook: not a mere black woman that does the cooking, but one bearing a patent stamped by the broad seal of Nature; the type of a class whose skill is not of books or training, but a gift both rich and rare." In this instance, a white woman claims that she can determine the culinary skill of the cook "just by looking at her" and that the cook has a God-given gift to prepare food. Reading these images relies upon a degree of knowledge, memory, and history that would have been common during the time of the magazine's publication. Indeed, race is the signifying element within these advertisements, and they all sought to tell the same story: Black women's talents are reserved for the domestic sphere, especially the kitchen.

CIVIL RIGHTS AND THE EMERGENCE OF SOUL

The mammy stereotype catalyzed some who believed that Black racial uplift required Black women to distance themselves from their culinary past and adopt "proper" expressions of cooking and eating. Indeed, the central tenet of the National Association of Colored Women's Clubs was racial uplift, and the politics of food was a by-product of these broader goals of activism.[28] The types of foods that poor and working-class Black women ate and the manner in which they ate them were sources of angst for many women in the Progressive Era. As such, it should not come as a surprise that these reformers would attempt to craft an image of Black women that contradicted the white gaze, which only saw mammy and her traditional foodstuffs.

Pioneering educator and women's rights activist Charlotte Hawkins Brown was one such reformer. Brown's writing on etiquette and social graces in a 1940 book entitled *The Correct Thing to Do, to Say, to Wear* was very much in keeping with the concerns held by many middle-class Black people regarding Blacks who were migrating from the South. Her instructional guide argues that acquiring particular graces and mannerisms would help African Americans be recognized as a people capable of fitting in within American society and, in so doing, would remove the objections to their presence in large numbers.[29] As such, her book featured menus for hosting formal and informal gatherings. It is interesting to note the total absence of chicken, pork chops, and other foods that one might racially link to African Americans and the presence instead of menu items such as chopped olive sandwiches and bonbons for informal teas and assorted canapés and frosted cakes for more formal gatherings.[30] As the Black middle class began to emerge, food became a culinary marker of the schism that existed—and arguably still exists—among classes of Black people. Cookbooks like Brown's are an example of how food became a platform for respectability politics; certain foods were understood to signify civility and respectability to society. In essence, Brown's program for racial uplift argued that if Black people desire to be accepted by white society, they should refrain from eating foods that white people have ideologically linked to an allegedly uncultured and unsophisticated barbaric African past.

During the mid-twentieth century, the civil rights movement played an important role in creating a Black identity capable of reaching across the emerging divide between middle-class and poor Blacks. Food was perhaps the most potent signifier of this growing divide. From an ideological standpoint, soul food could be interpreted in light of the civil rights movement itself. Historian Frederick Douglas Opie has researched the history and development of soul food by tracing African Indigenous culinary practices and connecting them with everyday food rituals practiced by Black people on both sides of the Atlantic. Opie writes that the language of Black soul began to emerge in popular culture in the 1960s when "African American urban dwellers, first in the Southeast and then in the Northeast, gradually made the transition from talking about rock music (rhythm and blues) and Southern food to call[ing] it soul music and soul food." "Soul" became a linguistic signifier for Black culture; it was shorthand for being able to survive in a racist society and a means of self-empowerment that undermined whites' definitions of social acceptability.[31] Soul ideology projected the notion that growing up Black and poor in a racist society gave Black people experiential wisdom that was uniquely powerful. This experiential wisdom was evident in the food that Black people (predominantly women during this period) prepared for their communities.

In relation to the civil rights movement, we should understand soul food to signify the reclaiming of a culinary identity based on principles that critique the white racist imagination projected upon Black people and their diets. More generally, soul food was the predominant cuisine of the Old South that Black people historically prepared, and Black people who had migrated North were nostalgic for food that reminded them of home. Dishes such as gumbo, hoppin' John, and pepper pot and their various ingredients are an essential part of this culinary tradition. The inexpensive cuts of meat that slaves and poor folks alike ate during the Reconstruction era were adopted as a part of the tradition: pig's feet, pig ears, spare ribs, and chitlins are among the most well-known of these food items.

To be sure, this description of soul food fed and continues to feed into the aforementioned class divide among Black people. However, the power of Black soul and soul food is evident in the fact that, for a period, this food was influential in creating spaces where socioeconomically diverse groups of Black people could gather over a meal and feel connected to their ancestral past, both real and imagined. While soul food remained the cuisine of choice for every poor person because it was inexpensive and signified Blackness, it also became the "revolutionary high cuisine of bourgeois African Americans."[32]

Nevertheless, the ideology that surrounded soul food began to shift in the 1970s, and the unifying characteristics of soul as a cultural signifier began to fade. Two reasons for the decline are particularly significant for our reimagination of soul food. The first was the growing influence of the Nation of Islam under the leadership of Elijah Muhammad. Muhammad's two-volume work *How to Eat to Live*, published in 1967 and 1972, respectively, describes soul food as "slave food." Muhammad advocated for a diet based on vegetables, fruit, and limited amounts of meat, but no pork. Muhammad also theorized that white people were behind the popularity of soul food as a means to eliminate Black people by eating themselves to death.[33] The lyrics of Goodie Mob at the beginning of this chapter demonstrate the staying power of this aspect of Muhammad's theory, namely, his skeptical view of white people promoting foods in Black communities.

The second reason for the ideological shift is that middle- and upper-class Black people continued to adopt dietary practices such as those encouraged by Charlotte Hawkins Brown. In order to be accepted by middle- and upper-class whites, some Black people distanced themselves from foods that could be stereotypically described as "Black food." During an interview with a self-described group of middle-class Black women, Williams-Forson recorded one interviewee who said that she would not eat chicken at her job because she "was not going to get but so Black at work." Yet when Williams-Forson asked a group of self-described lower-middle-class Black women about eating chicken at work and referenced the previous response, one person responded by saying that Williams-Forson was "dealing with high class" Black people who were "trying to act like they are better" than other Black people.[34]

These comments reveal the cultural tension that exists between and among food, class, and cultural identity within Black culture. The notion that the middle-class Black woman would only act "so Black" at work signifies that she probably acts (or feels free to act) "more Black" when among family and friends at home, thus fueling the belief held by many working-class Black people: that middle- and upper-class Black folks have "sold out" to whites for the sake of economic and social gain.[35]

As the power of soul food as a cultural signifier faded and the linguistic signifier of "soul" fell out of the popular vernacular, the growing class and cultural divide among Black people became more and more apparent. Though it mirrored a growing divide between middle-class and poor whites, this divide was particularly devastating for Black communities because it made it difficult for an already small minority to maintain the social solidarity necessary in order to resist the structural evil we have endured since colonial times.

To be sure, one of the reasons why the language of soul and soul food began to fade during the 1970s was due to the belief that soul food as such could only extend to the types of foods that slaves and poor Blacks ate, such as chitlins, hog maws, pig's feet, and fried chicken. However, I contend that this particular framing of soul food as fixed, static, and solely unhealthy is a product of the white fantastic imagination. In other words, many of the modern myths and ideologies that surround soul food have been interpreted and told through the lens of what sociologist Joe Feagin describes as the white racial frame.

The white racial frame is a worldview that interprets everything through the lens of the white experience. As the dominant worldview of Western society, it encompasses a "broad and persisting set of racial stereotypes, prejudices, ideologies, images, interpretations and narratives, emotions, and reactions to language accents, as well as racialized inclinations to discriminate."[36] Since the end of the Reconstruction era, the dominant Eurocentric culture has benefited from framing Black cookery and agricultural skill as something endowed upon Blacks by white people during enslavement. Black cookery has been projected as simple, unhealthy, worldly, and barbaric because the fantastic white imagination wanted to believe that Black people were simple-minded, unhealthy, worldly, and barbaric—more importantly, they wanted Black people to believe that description was accurate as well. The ideological projection of soul food as a by-product of Black ignorance with regard to our health and well-being is used to justify the racist inequities and outcomes in our food system and health care. As we will see in chapter 2, many corporations argue that they cannot operate in Black communities because there is not a demand for fresh and healthy food. This myth, along with the others mentioned earlier, reminds us that constructing liberatory Black foodways requires an exploration of slavery, Jane and Jim Crow segregation, and our contemporary eating habits as parts of an evolving African American culinary legacy.

GARDENING, COOKING, AND RECLAIMING OUR SOUL

By writing *In Search of Our Mothers' Gardens*, Alice Walker was able to promote the work of pioneering Black women writers such as Zora Neale Hurston and Phillis Wheatley, as well as provide a sense of literary continuity between those writers and herself.[37] Walker thus drinks from the wellspring of ancestral wisdom to ensure continuity of her womanist ethos and to create a model for personal and communal survival.

Emilie Townes suggests that "if there is no time or space or method in ethical discourse to ask crucial moral questions—Who is naming any of us? Who is making our history a denigrating mythological construction?—then we allow others, real others, to carve out hollow legacies for future generations of all color."[38] Given the fantastic white imagination's ideological construction of Black foodways, I believe that we have a responsibility to undermine these projections and, similar to what Walker does in her text, reclaim the culinary and agricultural wisdom of our ancestors.

Reclaiming and decolonizing Black foodways requires, among other things, that we delink from the ideologies projected upon Black foodways by the white fantastic imagination and craft new culinary and agricultural knowledges reflective of a more thorough understanding of our collective history. Reframing Black culinary traditions using ecowomanist ecomemories—again, not the rejection but the reconstitution of history—will enable us to be open to new epistemologies (i.e., ways of knowing) as they relate to Black agricultural practices and foodways.[39] This approach allows us to find agency in the stories of our ancestral farmers and Black cooks of the past to reclaim the garden and the kitchen as sacred spaces and conduits of sacred wisdom.

Chattel slavery ensured a lasting connection between African Americans and American soil. However, if we reframe the stories of those who worked in the fields to privilege the history of African farmers, we discover that our connection to agriculture does not begin or find its roots on plantations; instead, those roots are in the highly regarded agricultural skills of the West African cultures of our ancestral past. Recall that one of the primary reasons that West Africans were enslaved was their agricultural and animal husbandry prowess. Slaves carried different values in certain parts of the United States and the Caribbean, depending on where they originated. Slaves who were from the coastal area of the Niger River region were especially prized in South Carolina because they had intimate knowledge of Carolina's cash crop, rice. According to Harris, the variety of rice grown in South Carolina originated in the area that is known today as Senegambia, and it was cultivated by utilizing a uniquely African system of agriculture: "From the flooded alluvial plains where it was grown, to the system of dikes and sluiceways, to the system of assigning specific production-calibrated jobs to workers, Africa shows its hand on Carolina's rice cultivation." The Fulani, West Africans who lived along the Niger River regions of present-day Senegambia, Nigeria, and Mali, were well known for their

herding and husbandry. The herding and husbandry techniques that
become commonplace in the South and Southwest mirror the descriptions of herding in Fulani-occupied regions of West Africa.[40]

While many large plantations practiced the earliest forms of monoculture and accordingly grew tobacco, rice, indigo, and cotton in epic
proportions, they were also responsible for growing the varieties of
foods that fed their respective communities. On some plantations, the
masters either needed or allowed slaves to save and forage seeds to grow
their own food to supplement their food rations; this arrangement resulted in some slaves earning an income by selling excess food.[41] Many
of the plants that slaves grew in their gardens, such as okra, watermelon,
eggplant, and gourds, harked back to distantly remembered African
tastes. Some slaves were even able to grow enough food and catch
enough wild game that their masters purchased items from them.

Developing an awareness and appreciation of the agricultural knowledge that was latent in our African ancestors is essential if we are
going to recognize our interdependent relationship with our environments. By reframing the legacy of Black agriculture within the African
American community, farming and gardening can be seen as liberative
practices that promote food justice and reconnect us to a past that
goes beyond slavery. The skills of Black agricultural workers proved to
be both life-saving and soul-affirming by enabling them to maintain
a culinary connection to their African ancestors. By replanting in our
mothers' gardens and growing food, Black communities can begin to
create positive relationships with the land rather than adopting the
oppressive racist ideological project that framed Africans and their
ancestors as mere laborers rather than the wise farmers they obviously
were.

The ideological reconstruction of Black foodways for African Americans must also extend beyond agriculture and into the kitchen to
confront gender stereotypes. In recalling the story of Roy Hawkins, the
headwaiter of the Coon Chicken Inn, we discover that Black people
were agents and not merely victims of racial oppression as it relates to
food. Though some may question the logic of searching for expressions of Black self-determination from a man who would submit to
working in an environment that caricatured his very being, Hawkins's
story adds much-needed context regarding his choice of employer:

See I come from Texas, from a college town . . . Texas A&M. Back then
it was all men. They would catch a young Black boy and beat him up.
I'd hide anytime in the weeds. Who! I get out and hide like a rabbit.
See, that's what we had to endure. . . . Yeah, so people ask me how I
accepted [working at the Coon Chicken Inn]. Back in those days, coming from every part of the country . . . from southern places and things,
it wasn't nothing to see mockery. Black folks was always mocked. You
know you would see "Little Daisy" and "Sambo" on the lawn with the
water bucket. Those days we went on to work.[42]

Though Hawkins experienced constant mockery at his workplace, he
preferred suffering mockery while providing for his family to dying during the period of American history when Black men could be lynched.
While people may have laughed at him, he was "laughing all the way
to the bank," making upward of $100 in tips some nights.[43]

The story of Roy Hawkins reveals the difficult choice African Americans have to make in our struggle to obtain and maintain economic
self-determination. We can safely assume that Hawkins would have chosen another line of work if it had paid comparably. However, there are
certain conditions wherein one should be content with being as subver-
sive as one possibly can of dominant white culture without threatening
one's ability to survive. Although I am weary of the anthropocentric
projection of (nonhuman) animals upon Black people, in situations
such as his, we must do what we have to do in order to survive and
maintain control over our lives. Hawkins exemplifies such wisdom, and
his actions undermine the white fantastic imagination's projection that
Black men are only interested in chasing chickens and white women,
for he used chickens and the patronage of white women (and men)
to secure a stable life for his family.

Nevertheless, the kitchen has been a source of angst for many Black
people, most recently, Black women. This is due in part to the status
of cooking being seen as a "chore" within popular American culture.
The combination of cooking seen as a chore and the alignment of
Black women with food and mammy imagery has served to alienate
many women of color from their kitchens. However, as Townes notes,
the stereotypical racist image of the mammy is a mythological creation, a product of plantation legends, a representation that was never
as prevalent as we have been told.[44] The Black domestic workers in

southern white homes were often single and young and did not fit the stereotypical image of an older Black woman who loved tending to *her* white family.

Fighting against the mythology of mammy imagery thus requires that we delink from the ideological message that was constructed by the fantastic white imagination to reclaim the personhood of these women. I agree with Williams-Forson that "disregarding Black woman's cookery as a valued cultural work has greatly hindered [our] ability to see how food has been used for self-definition and self-valuation."[45] For instance, if we reexamine figure 8 and crop it such that the racist description of the woman is removed, we can see that this image does not convey anything personal about the woman, nothing about her culinary artistry, how much she might enjoy cooking for her family, or the fact that she even has a family. Perhaps this woman is such an excellent cook that she is able to sell some of the food she cooks and is saving to buy her or someone else's freedom. Indeed, rereading these images where the persons are seen as full human beings rather than victims creates a countermemory that empowers us to reclaim the Black experiential wisdom and self-determination embodied in these women. Furthermore, it also allows us to reclaim the knowledge cultivated by Black women cooks as a part of our ancestral legacy.

This legacy lives on in African American agricultural practices and our foodways. It is embedded in the soul of our community. Soul and soul food signify the commitment to remember our past, or to remember "the souls of Black folk," to borrow W. E. B. Du Bois's phrase, and a commitment to evolve with our futures, as those who coined the term "soul food" did during the civil rights movement. Given the legacy of the cultural significance of the terms "soul" and "soul food," I suggest that Black food justice activists view them as linguistic signifiers that encapsulate Black agricultural and culinary wisdom. Soul has deep religious and spiritual connotations, and Black folk have a spiritual relationship with the land and cooking that extends across the Atlantic and beyond slavery. From the milk rituals of Senegal and the yam celebrations in Nigeria to Black church potlucks, food has a spiritual significance in African and African American communities because Black foodways have always been tied to evolving definitions of Black identity and Black spirituality.

Figure 9. Black cook from *Harper's Weekly*, ca. 1856. Library of Congress.

Soul is the vivifying energy of our African and Black ancestors, an energy that lives within Black people. Soul is the experiential wisdom gleaned from foremothers and forefathers who taught African and African American people how to navigate in a foreign land. Soul is also surviving in the midst of oppression without losing sight of the ultimate goal of thriving. Soul signifies *faith* in, *hope* for, and *solidarity* with all Black people.

Soul has a decidedly affective dimension, power and influence that cannot be adequately expressed in language.[46] From the perspective of affect, *soul is what it feels like to be Black—what it feels like to be and believe in "us."* The affective dimension of soul offers Black people not only an acute sense of a felt us but also a particular affective configuration of us fashioned out of a particular set of affective materials: faith, hope, and solidarity.[47] In this way, soul as an affective ideological force is porous, given that what it feels like to have faith in, hope for, and solidarity with Black bodies shifts and changes over time, culture, and circumstances. The constant factor is that soulfull actions should uplift and empower Black communities.

The spirit of Black soul is one that pulls us toward an interdependent understanding of community by fashioning an antioppressive society where all planetary life flourishes. Understood this way, soul conveys the essence of Black spirituality and African American culinary and agricultural legacies. Soul enabled our ancestors to be critical of a nation that allegedly prized freedom while enslaving millions. It was the soul of our community that gave our ancestors the strength to resist Jane and Jim Crow segregation and lynching in their pursuit of civil rights. The soul of Black folk has always undermined white definitions of acceptability, because those definitions have historically been steeped in white supremacy. As such, soul enables us to reconstruct the culinary assumptions of soul food in ways that benefit our community.

By fully embracing the decolonial knowledge that is Black soul, we create room for our definition of soul food to evolve. Black American history is the history of a people who have had to adapt to the cultural, political, and economic hegemony of European American culture in order to survive. The traditional West African diet, which consisted of "darker whole grains, dark green leafy vegetables, and colorful fruits and nuts," supplemented with meat, was necessarily adapted during slavery.[48] It was the soul of Black folk postslavery that empowered Black people to adapt and develop an almost intuitive understanding of how to make something that other people were willing to throw away (like the aforementioned cuts of meat) taste wonderful. For the sake of our survival, Black foodways never had a static definition of what it means to eat in a way that is "Black" beyond eating in a way that enables one to survive, thrive, and flourish.

In this way, the evolution of soul food will only apply to the *types* of food that we prioritize eating. By this I mean to say that, in its truest sense, soul food is food that is prepared by members of our community who utilize the collective culinary wisdom of our ancestors to prepare meals that nourish the mind, body, and soul of those who partake in them. From this perspective, Black culinary cultural wisdom reveals that Black people like Roy Hawkins and Black women cooks have a unique ability to adapt and thrive in the midst of overwhelming oppression. Black spiritual wisdom reveals that their relationship to the land is not merely one of forced slave labor; it also includes agricultural intellectual ingenuity, from Senegal to South Carolina. This understanding of soul food not only pays tribute to our ancestors but also honors them by continuing to pursue freedom from oppression, a freedom they were ultimately denied.

COLLARD GREENS

Several years ago while I was volunteering for an after-school gardening club, one of the students whom I was trying to recruit to join the club asked a question that has lingered in my consciousness ever since. The Garden Club was one of only a few after-school activities that took place at the high school, and I wanted to try and recruit as many students of color to join as possible. After explaining to a young Black student what we would be doing—gardening, learning about food justice issues in California, and cooking—he looked at me and said, "What? Are you trying to make me a slave or something?"

At the beginning of this chapter I asked, What knowledges must be gained and retained and what must we let go of if we are to delink our foodways from coloniality and relink them into a just and sustainable food system? To be sure, the agricultural soil of America is covered in the blood, sweat, and tears of many forced laborers, among them African and African American slaves. The depth of psychological trauma embodied within us with respect to the enslavement and forced agricultural and culinary labor is profound.

How then do we work through this trauma? How might the young man recalibrate his feelings toward gardening? The answer is by developing a knowledge of ourselves that is delinked from coloniality and remembering that we too are created in the image of God. Self-love of this sort can help heal the ancestral trauma we carry when that love is expressed through self-compassion. Self-compassion asks us to pay attention to those feelings, to turn inward and cultivate a nonjudgmental awareness of the emotional stirrings within us that are activated when we think about farming or preparing food. It would be easy to judge the teenager for being hyperbolic, but doing so only strengthens the hegemonic white imagination, which begs us to forget and erase the evils of slavery. Paying attention, on the other hand, empowers us to seek to understand empathically the suffering that is hidden within the student's question. The suffering that animated his question is rooted in one or more of the following: fears, longings, aching wounds, and obstructed gifts.[49]

When we turn inward to understand empathically the suffering and the trauma within us when we discuss the forced enslavement of our ancestors an internal shift takes place—we are moved. We understand how the aching wounds of racism are still tied to agriculture and how those wounds have been handed down through generations to the student. We can also understand how reimagining Black foodways and agricultural and cooking practices challenges notions of Black identity in ways that trigger fear and longing: the fear of losing cultural authenticity and the longing to preserve a communal identity.

To be sure, understanding these wounds allows us to tend to them, to compassionately reassure the suffering inside of us until it feels fully seen, heard, held, and healed.[50] A more accurate understanding of the tragic past of African enslavement with respect to food and agriculture is an essential step along our path toward healing and wholeness with our relationships with the land and with cooking. The most critical and transformative learning I encountered in researching this book is that the story of our history with agriculture extends beyond slavery. We were an agricultural people, and many of us still feel the lure of gardening and farming in our bones. Embracing this legacy enabled me to discover a new love for the agricultural and culinary work of my ancestors.

In this way, decolonizing our knowledge of Black agriculture and foodways does not imply that we refuse to acknowledge the impact that slavery has had on our relationship with the land. Rather, decolonization requires (1) that we recognize that our agricultural history includes but is not limited to the enslavement of our ancestors; (2)

that we acknowledge the intellectual ingenuity of slaves rather than just complimenting their physical endurance and that we demand others to do so as well; (3) that we reject racist ideologies associated with Black foodways that uphold the fantastic imagination of white society; (4) that we delink our definition of soul food from the white racial frame to view soul food as a historically evolving set of foods that have physically, emotionally, and spiritually sustained Black people; and (5) that we construct countermemories to critique the white imagination and recast our ancestors as complex human beings rather than the less-than-human servants their enslavers understood them to be.

The second dish on our vegan soulfull table reminds me of the emotional complexities that are intertwined with our culinary identities and the difficulties we face when we delink our own imaginations from a fixed understanding of soul food. The first time I made citrus collard greens I was the senior pastor at First United Methodist Church of Compton, a predominantly Black and older congregation in Compton, California. My dietary preferences never came up while I was being interviewed for the job (why would they?!), and after I had been there only a few weeks, people were already noticing that I was not eating any meat.

Obviously, when I brought greens without any pig product to share the congregation realized that my diet wasn't the norm for most Black pastors. However, I knew that because I was the senior pastor of the church, the congregation would feel obligated to at least try my greens. Once they tasted them and realized that you could make greens without bacon, fatback, or any other nonhuman animal product, we began to have eye-opening conversations about how their diets have evolved and shifted over time. Interestingly, I learned that many of the older women rarely ate meat, especially red meat and pork, but didn't call themselves vegetarians because they believed the word was too associated with white dietary culture. The food on our plates and in our bowls has always informed whom we understand ourselves to be and what communities we belong to. The challenge that confronts us as Black people and people of faith is to be critical of the sources of our information so that our food might form us into the liberative antioppressive community we are called to become.[51]

Ingredients

coarse sea salt
2 pounds collard greens, chopped
1 tablespoon extra virgin olive oil
2 garlic cloves, minced
⅔ cup raisins
⅓ cup fresh orange juice

Directions

In a large pot over high heat, bring 3 quarts of water to a boil and add 1 tablespoon salt. Add the collards and cook, uncovered, for 8–10 minutes, until softened. Meanwhile, prepare a large bowl of ice water in which to cool the collards. Remove the collards from the heat, drain, and plunge them into the bowl of cold water to stop cooking and set the color of the greens. Drain by gently pressing the greens in a colander. In a large sauté pan, combine the olive oil and the garlic and raise the heat to medium. Sauté for 1 minute. Add the collards, raisins, and ½ teaspoon salt. Sauté for 3 minutes, stirring frequently. Add orange juice and cook for an additional 15 seconds or so. Be careful not to overcook, as the greens should be bright green in color. Season with additional salt to taste if needed and serve immediately. This recipe serves 5–6 people.

Chapter 2
Food Pyramid Scheme

I have called my tiny community [in Tennessee] a
world, and so its isolation made it; and yet there was
among us but a half-awakened common consciousness,
sprung from common joy and grief, at burial, birth or
wedding; from a common hardship in poverty, poor
land, and low wages; and above all from the sight
of the Veil that hung between us and Opportunity.
. . . The mass of those to whom slavery was a dim
recollection of childhood found the world a puzzling
thing: it asked little of them, and they answered with
little, and yet it ridiculed their offering.
—W. E. B. Du Bois, *The Souls of Black Folk*

The first thing you learn in the hog plant is the value
of a sharp knife. The second thing you learn is that you
don't want to work with a knife. Finally, you learn that
not everyone has to work with a knife. Whites, blacks,
American Indians and Mexicans, they all have their
separate stations. The few whites on the payroll tend
to be mechanics or supervisors. As for the [American]
Indians, a handful are supervisors; others tend to
get clean menial jobs like warehouse work. With few
exceptions, that leaves the blacks and Mexicans with
the dirty jobs at the factory, one of the only places
within a 50-mile radius in this muddy corner of North
Carolina where a person might make more than $8 an
hour.
—Charlie LeDuff, "At a Slaughterhouse, Some Things
   Never Die"

Regional and cultural preference plays an essential role in shaping what foods people believe they should be eating. Interrogating the ideologies that helped shape our contemporary notion of Black foodways helped us discern between the colonial ideologies of the racist white imagination and decolonial ideologies that can inform a vision of what food justice might look like for Black people. Having described how a decolonized understanding of our culinary and agricultural knowledge equips us to develop a more nuanced understanding of the development and importance of Black foodways and what we need to unlearn, we move on to applying these knowledges in a sociological analysis of the domestic and global food systems.

The second step in my decolonial method, thinking, seeks to enable marginalized people to examine themselves in relation to their own experiences and cultural histories. Thinking in this way allows us to take seriously the historical situation that gave rise to a contemporary injustice: the oppressive food politics in the United States, the impact of those policies on Black, Indigenous, and other people of color, and their impact on other parts of the world.

One question might emerge for some as we make this shift toward examining food systems: How are food and farmworker justice relevant to Black foodways and food justice for Black people? First, we must remember that the primary reason there are Black people in America is tied to African enslavement for the purposes of forced agricultural labor. Black foodways developed as they did in part as a consequence of the injustice endured by enslaved African farmworkers and their descendants. Exploring farmworker injustice allows us to see how a broken theological anthropology, racism, and coloniality continue to operate in the domestic food system after emancipation, Reconstruction, and civil rights. Indeed, much of our current food system was developed as a way to economically and politically marginalize Black people, Black labor, and other poor farmers.

For instance, the United States has enabled and arguably encouraged farmworker exploitation through the sanctioning of oppressive labor practices and through the denial of certain labor rights and protections to farmworkers. When these laws were passed, the vast majority of farmworkers were Black, and currently most farmworkers are people of color. Refusing to include agricultural laborers in the National Labor Relations Act of 1935 (which included provisions regarding the right to form unions), the Social Security Act of 1935, and the Fair Labor Standards Act of 1938 underscores the marginal status of farmworkers in US government and labor policy.[1]

Moreover, while Black people are no longer the dominant ethnic minority group working in agricultural fields, farmworkers and food workers are still overwhelmingly people of color. Most are paid wages that keep them impoverished, are food insecure, and experience nearly twice the level of wage theft as white workers: "While white food workers have an average annual income of $25,024, workers of color earn only $19,349 a year. White workers hold nearly 75 percent of the managerial positions in the food system. Latinos hold 13 percent and Black and Asian workers 6.5 percent."[2] In rural America, Black food workers have traded the field for the factory and work in concentrated animal feeding operations, commonly referred to as factory farms. As the *New York Times* article "At a Slaughterhouse, Some Things Never Die" illustrates, working in a factory farm is brutal on your mind and your body, as evidenced by the near 100 percent low-level employee turnover at this particular Smithfield packing plant.[3] The racial hierarchy that operated in this plant in 2000, when the article appeared, reflects the hierarchy of the plantations of the Old South, with the exception that in addition to Blacks, immigrant Latinx folks are being similarly exploited. As such, any argument for food justice for Black communities must examine and address farmworker and food worker injustice and its impact on Black and other people of color.

Second, recall that one aim of this book is to demonstrate how our food system is structurally racist. In order to make this argument, we must gain a basic understanding of how our food system operates on a structural level to expose the underlying assumptions that justify the health and access disparities and the environmental damage that continue to marginalize people of color. Our food system was designed to thrive upon initially a no-wage and eventually a low-wage labor force to help control the cost of goods. As Black people gained political rights in the 1960s, the oppression within this sector of the industrial food system shifted from African Americans to the Indigenous and Latinx immigrant communities. Within these communities we can see how the dehumanizing logics of coloniality and enslavement continue to inform agricultural practice in the United States, and in so doing, we can begin to discern ways to fight for food justice that are beneficial to Black and other exploited communities. For instance, the Coalition of Immokalee Workers (CIW), a worker-based human rights organization that is leading the fight to end human trafficking, modern-day slavery, and other labor abuses in agriculture, has documented nine cases of modern-day slavery within the US food system.[4] In one especially poignant case, Abel Cuello, who had held over thirty tomato pickers against their will in trailers in the swampland of Immokalee, Florida, used his vehicle to run over one of the workers who was trying to escape while stating that he *owned* them.[5]

What are the underlying assumptions that have permitted our current food system to develop in these ways that support human trafficking? How have the political policies of the food industry affected the well-being of farmers in the United States and around the world? What are the origins of these and other inequalities with regard to Black, Latinx, and poor people's access to food? How might compassion inform our thinking with regard to the suffering and exploitation of food workers and those guilty of exploitation? In our quest to think through answers to these questions, we will explore the political economy (e.g., the interdisciplinary study of production, trade, law, and economics) of food production as it relates to African Americans, the domestic poor, and the global poor. In doing so, we will survey the impact of two significant food policy agencies, The United States Department of Agriculture (USDA) and the World Trade Organization (WTO), and explore the role multinational corporate practices play in food security and sovereignty of communities of color.[6]

THE DOMESTIC POLITICS OF FOOD AND INFLUENCE

Food production, distribution, and consumption are political issues. The domestic agency tasked with wrestling with the politics of food is the USDA, which was founded in 1862 by President Abraham Lincoln as the Bureau of Agriculture. The bureau was initially described as the "people's department" because the agriculture industry employed over 50 percent of Americans, and Lincoln wanted the organization to serve the interests of the agricultural sector.[7] The bureau became a cabinet-level position in 1889 (hence the name change) and expanded its jurisdiction beyond its initial scope to become the third-largest branch of government after the Departments of Defense and the Interior.[8]

From the early 1900s until the New Deal era of the 1930s, the USDA operated with a balanced approach to its policies. On the one hand, it was supportive of the shift toward industrial agriculture, which mirrored other thriving industries such as the automobile industry. On the other hand, the USDA was responsive to the social concerns raised by grassroots agricultural organizations and allowed such organizations to participate in the development of USDA policies. The Great Depression (1929–39) brought a severe decline to the American economy, and the depression hit the rural economy particularly hard. The New Deal policies were introduced at a time when farmers were looking to the government for help in maintaining their livelihood, and the government was looking to farmers to ensure that they would produce enough food to feed all Americans. Through a combination of price supports for farm crops, rural electrification, and a stimulus plan to revive rural economies, the New Deal brought about a significant overhaul of federal farm policy.[9] Consequently, the USDA's role in developing domestic economic policy increased substantially.

The aftermath of World War II brought about a shift in agricultural practices due in part to the "leftover" chemicals that the American military developed for use in chemical warfare. After World War II the government encouraged munitions manufacturers to convert their products into fertilizer and pesticides; these substances included ammonium nitrate, the main ingredient in both bombs and chemical fertilizer.[10] The use of chemical fertilizers and pesticides laid the groundwork for an increase in concentrated farming practices such as monocultures rather than crop rotation and increased agricultural exports. Two secretaries of agriculture, Ezra Taft Benson (1953–61) and Earl Butz (1971–76), played critical roles in reshaping the USDA to focus on large *agribusiness* firms rather than *agriculture*, and much of their work was accomplished through reorganizational policies within the farm bill.

The first farm bill, the Agricultural Adjustment Act of 1933, was born out of the crisis that many farmers faced as a result of the Great Depression. Farmers were struggling to stay in business, banks were

foreclosing on their loans, prices for crops were so low that farmers were losing money on the crops they planted, and entire rural
economies were being devastated by the crash of the stock market.[11]
In response, the Agricultural Adjustment Act created policies that
would help rebuild the farm economy, such as pricing regulations,
soil conservation, and programs designed to disperse surplus growth
to community and school feeding programs. The reauthorization of
the act in 1948 laid the groundwork for commodity food assistance
to become a permanent component of the farm bill. It is also worth
noting that while Congress phased some social welfare programs out
of the initial bill, the National School Lunch Program, which was also
designed to combat nationwide hunger, was made permanent within
the bill in 1946.

During the 1950s, the USDA (under Secretary Benson) began encouraging the mechanization of farm production with the goal of producing surplus commodities that could be used to penetrate foreign
markets. At the same time, according to food justice activists Robert
Gottlieb and Anupama Joshi, the USDA established farm bill policies
that encouraged the rise of nonfarm food producers and marketers
but seemingly ignored the increasing loss of small farms as they were
absorbed into more concentrated landholdings. During this period,
the country witnessed a shift where California, with its more "modern" industrial approaches to agriculture, surpassed Iowa to become
the nation's leading agriculture-producing state. Because the farms
of central California were commercially owned, the state's increasing
agricultural landscape embodied what USDA secretary Benson referred
to as agribusiness. He saw agribusiness as "all operations performed in
connection with the handling, storage, processing, and distribution of
farm commodities."[12] Benson viewed agribusiness as a market-driven
approach to agriculture and argued that by using this model the United
States would eventually eliminate federally supported food production
and distribution.

However, farm bill policies have not been able to eliminate commodity subsidies in some shape or form. Through the farm bill, the USDA
now uses crop insurance to subsidize the cost of commodity crops such
as corn, soybeans, and rice and encourages overproduction. This policy
results in cheap grain that farmers can sell below cost due to financial

subsidies from the government. Consequently, the flood of cheap grain eventually works its way through the food system and drives "down the price of all the calories derived from that grain: the high-fructose corn syrup in the Coke, the soy oil in which the potatoes were fried, the meat and cheese in the burger."[13] During the era of USDA secretary Butz (the 1970s), the focus on international trade increased as the USDA began subsidizing grain trading companies such as Cargill and Archer Daniels Midland. By the early 1980s, those companies, along with other emerging food corporations, were essentially writing the farm bill and ensuring a steady supply of cheap commodity crops that they could trade internationally and process into the types of value-added crops and products previously described.[14]

In the midst of the USDA's shift from agriculture to agribusiness, it was given food-related social welfare programs to administer in addition to the National School Lunch Program. The Supplemental Nutrition Assistance Program (SNAP), known as "food stamps"; the Special Supplemental Nutrition Program for Women, Infants, and Children (WIC); and the Temporary Emergency Food Assistance Program (TEFAP) became components of the farm bill and thus were administered by the USDA from the 1970s through the 1990s. Agribusiness corporations welcomed the addition of these programs as a way to increase sales of their surplus crops. An apt description of the mission of the USDA that took shape during this period would be to feed the poor and feed the schoolchildren, but do it with the surplus commodity crops and surplus meat and dairy products. In other words, the current mission of the USDA is at best to address the interests of both agribusiness and those who are dependent on the aforementioned social welfare programs and at worst to prioritize the interests of the agribusiness farm lobby.

The farm lobby includes farm organizations such as the American Farm Bureau Federation, which represents most commercial farmers and is predominantly Republican; the National Farmers Union, which represents the interests of smaller farmers and is mostly Democrat; and a host of other private lobby organizations such as the National Corn Growers Association and the National Cotton Council of America. The corporate farm lobby has gained undue influence in policy-making due to what sociologist and nutritionist Marion Nestle terms "the revolving door" of food lobbyists and government officials.[15] To be sure, the American political system has a long history of accepting lobbying as an integral part of the political process, and lobbying itself is not the problem in this instance. Rather, it is the conflict of interest that occurs within the USDA when, as Nestle points out, "lobbyists and government officials are not always distinct populations. Today's public servant is tomorrow's lobbyist and vice versa."[16]

The revolving door between corporate food lobbyists and government officials has been especially prevalent within the USDA, where approximately five hundred agency- and staff-related positions are political appointments subject to party affiliation. For example, in 1971 the secretary of agriculture, Clifford Hardin, and the director of Ralston Purina, Earl Butz, *literally traded places*, with Butz becoming the new secretary and Hardin becoming the new director of Purina. In another case, the chief USDA negotiator, who arranged for private companies to sell grain to the Soviet Union in 1972, resigned upon completion of the negotiation to work for the corporation that gained the most from the transaction.[17]

Donald Trump's selection of Sonny Perdue as his secretary of agriculture in 2017 demonstrates that the revolving door between agribusiness and agricultural regulation shows no sign of slowing down. Purdue is the founding partner of Purdue Partners LLC, which primarily operates within the agribusiness sector.[18] Purdue grew up on a farm in Georgia before rising to the office of governor in his home state. During his tenure as governor, he was named Governor of the Year by Biotechnology Innovation Organization (a genetically modified organism lobbying firm) because of his strong advocacy of the biosciences in Georgia.[19] Shortly after he began his tenure as secretary of agriculture, the USDA "abruptly removed inspection reports and other information from its website about the treatment of animals at thousands of research laboratories, zoos, dog breeding operations and other facilities."[20] While one could argue that government officials from the USDA bring invaluable expertise to the corporations that hire them and are often a great help for corporations attempting to work through regulatory policy to market new products, the same cannot be said of the reverse. The practice of recruiting industry executives to government work raises questions of conflict of interest because, given these executives' recent history, it is increasingly difficult to argue that USDA legislation benefits consumers, particularly consumers who are people of color or poor, more than agribusiness.[21]

According to Robert Paarlberg, besides buying its way into political office as a means to craft policy, the farm lobby secures its influence in regard to agriculture policy (especially the farm bill) through its financial support of members of the House and Senate agriculture committees. These organizations contribute to the reelection campaign of their favorite members or fund other candidates who the organizations believe can challenge committee members who have not voted in their interests. Currently, the farm lobby wields a tremendous amount of influence in policy, as displayed in the 2008 farm bill debate. In 2008 net farm income reached $89 billion, 40 percent above the average of the previous ten years. Despite this, the farm lobby successfully argued that it needed additional safety net protection in the form of additional subsidies to prevent unforeseen "emergencies." As a result, in 2011 and 2012 farm income levels in the United States were the highest and second-highest on record and would have been so even without the increased subsidies.[22]

While at first glance it may appear that eliminating or lowering the safety net subsidies would be a helpful move, given the record increases in net farm income, this is neither an ideal nor a practical solution. A careful analysis of the farm bill by Vincent Smith in 2016 revealed that 15 percent of farm operations received 85 percent of federal funding. Smith, professor of economics at Montana State University, describes this practice as "crony capitalism," in which large corporate farms have successfully lobbied congressional representatives to continue a program that was initially designed to aid relatively small family farms. To be sure, the corporate farming industry projects the idea that farm subsidies are necessary in order to prevent small family farms from going out of business or from going into poverty in their desire to put food on America's tables. However, small farms often receive little or no help from the programs approved and run by Congress.[23]

Consequently, given the pragmatic stresses of farming (i.e., unpredictable weather, pests, plant diseases, etc.) and the current economic stress of a system seemingly rigged against them, farmers are increasingly committing suicide in the United States.[24] Sadly, in 2016 the

Centers for Disease Control and Prevention released a study showing that people working in agriculture, including farmers, farm laborers, ranchers, fishers, and lumber harvesters, take their lives at a higher rate than any other occupation in the United States.[25] To be sure, the United States is not the only country facing an increase in farmer suicide. European, Asian, and African farmers are taking their own lives as well.

We must ask ourselves why, given the size of the farm bill (about $956 billion), Congress does not allocate some funding for mental health services to address the epidemic of farmer suicides? In the late 1980s, in response to a similar increase in farmer suicides, Congress did fund programs designed to provide mental health care to farmers. Mike Rosmann, a psychologist and farmer, began the Farm and Ranch Stress Assistance Network (FRSAN) and received some federal funding.[26] Unfortunately, while Congress included the program in the 2008 farm bill, no funding was allocated for it. The 2014 version of the bill did not provide any funding either, and Congress again chose to stifle the outreach capacity of the FRSAN program. Indeed, in the farm bill's 2014 iteration, the Republican-controlled Congress voted to decrease funding for *public entitlement* programs such as WIC and food stamps in order to help offset the fiscal impact *corporate entitlements* in the form of farm subsidies would have on our national deficit. As a result, the concerns of poor people, farmers or otherwise, are overlooked for the sake of corporate profit and campaign contributions. The USDA's treatment of small family farms is one among many examples that illustrate how the department has not been fairly representing the needs of consumers, especially poor consumers, or of those who rely on social welfare programs. However, the USDA's treatment of Black farmers is the strongest example of unfair policy, racism, and discrimination that harms consumers and communities.

Black people were meant to be tillers of the land but never owners—this has been the overarching sentiment held by the USDA toward Black farmers. It is a racist projection of the hegemonic white imagination that frames Blacks as capable farm laborers but as too ignorant to manage the large-scale farms that drive our current food system. From the end of the Reconstruction era until today, federal, state, and local governments have enforced racist policies and implemented racist practices that have nearly eliminated all Black farmers in the United States.

At the end of Reconstruction, Black people found themselves working agriculture as their primary source of employment, mostly as sharecroppers or tenant farmers. Sharecropping is but a stone's throw away from slavery. While tenants are not enslaved, they farm land that they do not own for the promise of splitting the profits generated from the crops they raised. Given the necessity of money for day-to-day living, most tenant farmers borrowed money from the landowners to remain financially stable until the harvest. However, this practice led to most farmers finding themselves in an endless cycle of debt, having to work the land for woefully inadequate wages they had already been paid and spent.

Despite the immense challenges of owning land and farming in post-Reconstruction America, Black southern agrarians were determined to own land to gain a measure of self-determination. In 1900 Black southerners owned 158,479 farms, and by 1910 that number had increased to nearly 200,000 and totaled more than 15 million acres of land.[27] The number of Black farmers peaked at 926,000 in 1920, and they owned over 16 million acres of land.[28] Unfortunately, the Great Depression, the resulting New Deal policies, and, eventually, the obstructionist practices of the USDA have led to a steep decline in Black farmers and landownership.

As discussed above, farmers were in a perilous state during the Great Depression, and the New Deal policies were needed to keep them afloat in order to ensure sufficient food production to feed the country. Unsurprisingly, the New Deal programs were administered in ways that prioritized white farmers and large landowners over everyone else. Three programs within the New Deal are worth noting. First, the Agricultural Adjustment Administration developed policies wherein local county committees allocated funds to needy farmers and their farmworkers. These committees were made up of white farmers who failed to disperse funds to tenants despite being legally required to do so.[29] The Farm Security Administration, which was responsible for assisting poor rural Americans, marginalized Black farmers by preventing them from using any money they did receive to purchase land. Lastly, the Standard Rural Rehabilitation Loan Program denied Black farmers credit or charged them obscene interest rates to borrow money; thus, Black farmers were unable to afford to mechanize their farms in the ways that the USDA increasingly demanded. The discriminatory lending practices of the USDA were so heinous that by 1982 Black farmers had only received 1 percent of all ownership loans, 2.5 percent of all farm operating loans, and 1 percent of all water conservation loans.[30] In total, of all government farm payments given to farmers, 97.8 percent of them went to white farmers, who received an average of $10,022 per farm, while the few Black farmers who did receive loans were on average given only $5,509 per farm.[31]

The racist lending policies of the USDA were brought to light in dramatic fashion in the landmark class action lawsuit *Pigford v. Glickman*. The plaintiffs, Timothy Pigford and four hundred other Black farmers, alleged that the USDA discriminated against Black farmers in its decisions to allocate price support loans, disaster payments, farm ownership loans, and operating loans.[32] Moreover, the plaintiffs also argued that the USDA had failed to process subsequent civil rights complaints about racial discrimination and actively sought to obstruct such complaints from being made. After the USDA initially denied the claims and decided to go to trial to fight the class action suit, internal USDA studies revealed a history of racial discrimination that prompted the agency to move toward mediation and settlement. The settlement, reached in 1999, awarded $1 billion in cash relief, debt relief, and tax relief to approximately twenty-three thousand class members. In February 2010 Attorney General Eric Holder announced an additional settlement of $1.25 billion, known as Pigford II, for an additional sixty-six thousand class members who were either unaware that they were eligible to participate in the previous lawsuit or too late to join. Despite these settlements, many Black farmers have had their applications for financial relief rejected. Unsurprisingly, the exact number of farmers to have received compensation has been a contentious issue and raised concerns of further discrimination, since nearly 50 percent of Pigford II claims and 30 percent of the initial Pigford claims have been rejected.

Despite the positive result of the Pigford cases, Black agrarians are still relatively rare in the United States. Currently, fewer than twenty thousand farmers are Black, a 98 percent decrease from the high in the 1920s, and these farmers own less than two million acres of land.[33]

To be sure, massive urbanization and the mechanization of farming have impacted the total number of farmers across all racial categories, yet white farmers only saw a 65 percent decrease during the same time span. It seems that the USDA still believes that Black people were meant to be tillers of the land but never landowners, and it is doing its part to keep this racist practice in place.

THE INTERNATIONAL POLITICS OF FOOD AND INFLUENCE

From an international perspective, the political economy of food began taking its current form in the late 1970s during the global economic recession. Before this period, countries in the Global South, including Africa and Asia, were borrowing money from banks that were flush with cash from oil-exporting countries to finance their oil imports. However, the recession caused interest rates to soar and set these countries on the path to bankruptcy. They soon found themselves stuck between a rock and a hard place, needing to borrow money to repay loans. Traditional lending sources were practically eliminated because of the increased risk of a loan default (i.e., these countries' poor credit). As a result, many of these indebted countries turned to internationally financed institutions for help, most notably, the World Bank.

Raj Patel, an Indian food justice activist, argues that "the mechanics of setting up a global food system involved the twin process of colonization and the forced creation of markets."[34] The lending policies of the World Bank forced an ideological colonization upon loan recipients: they implemented industrial agricultural practices because they were told that industrialization was the only method by which they could solve or prevent food shortages. This was a lie. In addition to the ideological colonization of industrialized agriculture, the World Bank forced the agriculture sector of these countries to be exposed to the "free market" without the safety nets of pricing guarantees that US and European Union food producers enjoy.

Historically, to borrow money from the World Bank, countries had to agree to a series of conditions known as structural adjustment programs. In many cases, according to Patel, the conditions attached to the loans involved making profound changes to each country's domestic economy, such as preventing the government from running a deficit, allowing currency to float freely on the international market, liberalizing trade, reducing or eliminating tariffs, and eliminating domestic support for farmers (i.e., guaranteeing a minimum price for products). The currency and agricultural mandates were especially problematic for developing countries. When a country allowed its currency to float freely on the market it was consistently devalued, which meant that domestic goods produced within developing countries were cheaper for foreign nations to buy, while foreign-produced goods became more expensive. Thus, it became more economically viable for developing countries with the right climate and soil conditions to incentivize farmers to abandon traditional agricultural practices and attempt to industrialize in order to grow food for the United States, the European Union, and other nations with more developed international economies rather than focusing on improving infrastructure to grow food for themselves. The former nations who had previously colonized these territories accordingly "managed to replace the old colonial instruments of command and control with newer, and cheaper, mechanisms of 'self-imposed' market discipline."[35] The agricultural model described in this paragraph is the current food production, distribution, and consumption model upon which the United States currently feasts.

Creating and maintaining this "new food order" for the globe requires political clout beyond the US government and the World Bank; indeed, this could not have happened without the emergence of the World Trade Organization (WTO). Through the post–World War II era, the General Agreement on Tariffs and Trade (GATT) was the primary legislative document that coordinated import/export taxes on industrial goods. The goal of GATT was to reduce taxes and tariffs on industrial goods that the participating nations traded with each other. When the global recession of the 1970s hit, many countries began to protect their national industries by shortcutting the tariffs; however, the US government persuaded the participating countries to go back to the bargaining table in 1984.

Although it took more than ten years, in 1995 the WTO emerged as the product of those meetings. The WTO inherited the core agreements of GATT, but it also "had new domains of expertise—intellectual property, services, textiles, agriculture, and crucially, it had new mechanisms for the resolution of disputes that gave the WTO the teeth that the US found so sorely lacking in GATT."[36] What is especially shocking and problematic for farmers in Africa, Asia, and Latin America is that the United States and the European Union were able to negotiate an agreement that allowed them to continue to subsidize their own farmers while other nations agreed to abdicate this form of agricultural support. Countries within Africa, Asia, and Latin America chose instead to allow large agribusiness corporations to invest private capital into their developing agricultural sector. Among the consequences of GATT and the subsequent agreements ushered in by the era of corporate-controlled food systems are that it placed many farmers in unprecedented amounts of debt and, as we shall see, has contributed to staggeringly high suicide rates.

The corporate-controlled food system emerged in the 1980s when global governance of food became dominated by international financial originations such as the World Bank, the International Monetary Fund, and the WTO. As previously noted, during this era, rules were put in place that pushed Western definitions of development upon emerging economies by opening up their markets to foreign investment and reducing or eliminating tariffs. While these policies were being crafted during the 1980s, the United States began to experience tremendous growth of corporate ownership in the food system. And with increased ownership came increased control and influence upon global food decision-making.

Under the corporate food system, "cheap food depends on the union of North Atlantic grains and southern fruits, vegetables, and seafood in an international division of agricultural labor coordinated by transnational corporate supply chains, with trade relations governed by institutions such as the World Bank and the WTO." To be sure, food produced within this supply chain can only be described as "cheap" from an American or European point of reference. Within this system, transnational agrifood corporations can exert enormous influence within three strategic segments of the global food system: food production, trade in both agricultural commodities and food processing, and food retailing.[37] In this way, multinational corporations such as Cargill are able to control portions of the food system from field to fork: they can buy, mill, and ship grain, feed it to livestock, and then supply the animal products to supermarkets. Cargill and other vertically integrated agrifood companies are therefore able to shield themselves from the volatility of the "free market," where prices are negotiated between various actors in the market, because the price of their commodities is mostly internal.

Corporations find themselves in this fortuitous position because they have been influential in crafting public opinion and public policy. The contentious issue of labeling GMO (genetically modified organism) products is perhaps the most noteworthy campaign by corporations to influence public opinion. In 2012 voters in the state of California were deciding whether or not to label foods that contain GMOs. As a resident of California during that time, I recall seeing a modest amount of both pro- and antilabeling marketing throughout the summer and fall months. However, as the vote drew near and polls showed that the referendum was likely to pass, corporate donors made a last-minute investment of $44 million for what they termed "voter education," which ultimately swung the decision in their favor. While the effort to shape public opinion is most evident in situations such as GMO labeling, corporations have been steadily increasing their influence in the agricultural research taking place at land-grant universities.

Beginning with their creation in 1862, land-grant universities have worked with local farmers to develop innovative agricultural methods and various types of seeds that were publicly available to all farmers.[38] However, since the 1980s federal policies have been developed that enabled the private sector to partner with land-grant schools to develop agricultural products and seeds that have ultimately led to the seed-patenting system that we see in our food system today. By 2010 nearly 25 percent of all agricultural research at the university level was funded by the private sector. This funding not only steers research to the goals of the for-profit sector but also discourages research that would be critical of our current agricultural-industrial model and "diverts public research capacity away from important issues such as rural economies, environmental quality and the public health implications of agriculture."[39]

In regard to public policy, the influence of and revolving door between corporate executives and government regulatory positions described in previous sections apply to international food regulatory bodies as well. According to Nora McKeon, corporations have an increasingly important role in food regulation through the rise of private standards and the decline of the government's regulatory role. For instance, the US delegation to the 2013 FAO-WHO Codex Alimentarius (the body that sets the standards applied by the WTO for trade in food products) was composed of nine people, five of whom were from corporations, and none of whom were representatives from consumer or farmer organizations.[40] By preventing small-scale farmers from participating in policy-making, corporations can force their program of industrialization and monoculture upon the majority of food producers who desire to enter the market. This has led to farmers needing to take out loans to "modernize" their farms in order to compete in their local markets or to secure a contract with a global agrifood corporation such as Archer Daniels Midland or Cargill. Unfortunately, these loan programs have not been as successful as farmers hoped they would be and have created a system of debt that has ravaged farmers in developing countries.

Many farmers in developing countries who are in debt used their first loans to invest in cash crops and land. At the urging of their governments and agribusiness seed corporations, farmers were told to embrace the entrepreneurial spirit of capitalism. This policy encouraged farmers to move away from their traditional polyculture practices (i.e., growing multiple varieties of crops) in order to adopt the intensive methods of monoculture. Farmers began to grow plants that they believed they could sell on the market, such as cotton, groundnut, rice, and sugarcane. However, because the WTO agreements prevent government subsidization, the farmers were subject to the whims of the market, which often changed, at times leaving them with crops that could not be sold. In other words, globalizing the market has practically transferred control of farming from the farmer to those who can shape the market.[41] If we recall that the WTO policies also liberalized local currencies, making these cash crops significantly cheaper than they were prior to the agreement, we realize that these farmers are caught in a vicious cycle of debt and hunger, having chosen to dedicate all of their lands to the WTO's free-market ideology of cash crops.

This cycle of debt has created a sense of despair and hopelessness among many farmers; consequently, similar to the United States, there

has been an epidemic of farmer suicides around the world, particularly in developing regions within Africa and India. For example, in
South Africa, the suicide claims for insurers increased by 20 percent in
2016 and has been attributed to farmer suicides.[42] The state of Andhra
Pradesh in India, which has a population in the millions, has been re-
cording rural suicide rates in the thousands. Punjab, the epicenter of
the agricultural biotechnology revolution (i.e., the Green Revolution),
has seen a dramatic increase in suicide rates. Some farmers in India
have resorted to selling their kidneys; others have even put themselves
up for sale as indentured servants. In Sri Lanka, "averaged out over the
country, pesticide poisoning (a common form of suicide among poor
farmers with easy access to chemical fertilizers) was the sixth leading
cause of death" in the country's hospitals—it is the leading cause of
death in rural hospitals.[43] Indeed, between 1996 and 2000, half of Sri
Lanka's recorded suicides were agricultural workers.

ENVIRONMENTAL RACISM

The brief analysis of how our food system has developed over the last
150 years gives us the context to begin thinking through our observa-
tions. Now we are able to return to one of our initial questions in the
chapter: What are the underlying assumptions that have allowed our
current food system to marginalize Black folks, people of color domestically and globally, and poor people around the world? I suggest
that at least two underlying assumptions that frame the global food
system are race and racism. As a part of the American racial project, the
global food system enables the dominant European American culture
to preserve power by limiting the access of African Americans, people
of color, and the global poor to the economic and political power that
could prevent these abuses.

To be sure, there are some food justice activists who might argue
that, given the social construction of race, class analysis alone offers
a better interpretive lens for considerations of systemic oppression
within the food system. While I agree that class is an essential component of any thoroughgoing analysis, there are two problems with this
color-blind approach to social analysis. First, it fails to recognize the
ideological power of coloniality as it has developed over the course

of nearly five hundred years of diffusion and enforcement as a funda-mental principle of social organization and identity formation. The longevity of the race concept and the enormous effects of the American racial project, which simultaneously interprets, represents, or explains racial identities and meanings "in an effort to organize and distribute resources along particular racial lines," almost guarantees that race will remain a feature of social reality.[44] Second, a color-blind approach fails to recognize that, on the level of lived experience, race is a part of everyone's identity, and one cannot just choose to be raceless. From such a perspective, to be without a racial identity is to be in danger of having no identity at all. As a consequence of the American racial project, *everyone* in the United States learns both consciously and un-consciously how to interpret his or her existence along the lines of racial classification.

When understood this way, the resulting racism that plagues our food system becomes much clearer. As a part of the American racial project, the food system has been organized to prioritize the distribu-tion of resources along the racial lines of whiteness. As a result, our food system can be described as structurally racist because it creates and reproduces structures of domination and marginalization based on racial significations and identities.[45] When compared to white people, Black, Indigenous, and other people of color have less access to food, and the food they can access is likely less nutritious. Farmers of color, especially those in the Global South, are disproportionately suffer-ing when compared to white American and European farmers due to neoliberal trade policies that have helped contribute to the failures of many postcolonial governments. Given that all human beings need food to survive, acknowledging the racism within our domestic and global food system helps us see how the lives and livelihoods of people of color are at stake. The fight for food justice, for the creation of food sovereign spaces, and environmental justice may well be a fight for our very lives.

The reorganization and redistribution of food resources in ways that marginalize Black people and the global poor, who are dispropor-tionately people of color, are forms of environmental racism. Indeed, when it comes to environmental policy, all communities are not cre-ated equal, particularly if we take into account the material wealth of a community and the ecological footprint that surrounds it. From an environmental analytical standpoint, the inequality of particular communities is made evident in that environmental regulations have not uniformly benefited all segments of society. Historically, people of color have had to contend with the by-products of municipal land-fills, hazardous waste treatment plants, and other polluting industries within their communities.[46] Why do some communities suffer through environmental degradation while others do not? Why are some work-ers protected from hazardous waste while others are not? I contend that the pervasive reality of racism should be at the very center of an adequate analysis of environmental degradation in general and food injustice in particular.

Environmental sociologist Robert Bullard's publications show how the pervasive reality of racism has played a crucial factor in environ-mental planning and policy-making and that governmental, legal, economic, political, and military institutions reinforce environmental racism. While Bullard admits that communities of color made some progress during the civil rights movement of the 1960s, this progress was short-lived. White people continue to control the majority of politi-cal power in the United States; as a result, new ways to skirt such policies and to continue to pollute impoverished areas followed in the wake of progress. For instance, in the greater Los Angeles area, 71 percent of blacks and 50 percent of Latinos live in the areas where there is the most polluted air, while only 34 percent of the white population does.[47] The trend in the greater Los Angeles area mirrors the national trend. Researchers Leslie Wernette and Dee Nieves note: "Out of the whole population [of the United States], a total of 33% whites, 50% blacks, and 60% Latinos live in the 136 counties in which two or more air pollutants exceed standards. The percentage living in the 29 counties designated as nonattainment areas for three or more pollutants are 12% white, 20% black, and 31% Latino."[48]

Many well-intentioned people—even liberal environmentalists—are hesitant to accept this assertion and would rather believe that this infor-mation is either exaggerated or somehow mistaken. However, in regard to environmental policy, what is being played out in Black communities is a result of racism and the lack of social and economic capital. A report prepared by Cerrell Associates for the California Waste Management

Board (CWMB) offers a detailed policy regarding factors that the CWMB should take into consideration for the placement of waste incinerators. The report states that all socioeconomic groups resist and resent waste facilities in their neighborhoods, "but the middle and upper socioeconomic strata possess better resources to effectuate their [incinerators'] position. Middle and higher socioeconomic strata neighborhoods should not fall within the one-mile to five-mile radius of the proposed site."[49] The recommendation for the placement of the incinerator had nothing to do with the environmental stability or soundness of the area but everything to do with the community's access to power.

Of course, environmental racism is not merely a domestic problem. Imperialism, colonialism, and multinational corporations have exported the domestic policy of environmental oppression to the global poor. International trade agreements crafted through GATT and WTO have created a framework wherein the United States and other imperial countries export their environmental practices to the rest of the so-called undeveloped world. When domestic communities of color began to organize and take legal action against dumping waste or pollution, American corporations chose to transport this waste to developing countries. More often than not, this practice is what environmental activists refer to as environmental job blackmail, when corporations promise to bring jobs to a city by building a waste disposal plant.[50] These jobs are always low-paying, and because many countries do not have the same emissions standards as the United States, the jobs end up costing the community more money than they generate due to increased health expenses incurred by the employees, as well as by the community surrounding the plant.

Economists and politicians refer to these practices as development to portray their motives as ones that are in the best interest of the "undeveloped" nation. However, a leaked document from the World Bank's chief economist, Lawrence Summers, shows that these economists and politicians are not as altruistic as they would have us believe. Summers wrote that there are three reasons why the World Bank should encourage "dirty" industries to migrate to less developed countries (LDCs):

  * The measurement of the costs of health impairing pollution depends on the foregone earnings from increased morbidity and

mortality. From this point of view a given amount of health impairing pollution should be done in the country with the lowest
cost, which will be the country with the lowest wages. I think the
economic logic behind dumping a load of toxic waste in the lowest
wage country is impeccable and we should face up to that.

* I've always thought that under-populated countries in Africa are
  vastly UNDER-polluted, their air quality is probably vastly ineffi-
  ciently low compared to Los Angeles or Mexico City.

* The demand for a clean environment for aesthetic and health
  reasons is likely to have very high-income elasticity. The concern
  over an agent that causes a one in a million change in the odds of
  prostate cancer is obviously going to be much higher in a country where people survive to get prostate cancer than in a country
  where under 5 mortality is 200 per thousand.[51]

This document sparked a significant controversy within the World
Bank and in the communities of First World countries as they began
to realize the pervasiveness of environmental racism.

From a global standpoint, the framework of environmental racism
reveals how European American colonialists implemented the logic
of a racial formation project within the respective colonial contexts.
The citizens of developing countries did not possess the political state-
sanctioned power to resist the implementation of policies that would
usher in a new era of hunger never before seen in fertile places such as
India and sub-Saharan Africa. The logic of racial formation combined
with the power of international state-sanctioned agencies such as the
WTO begin to explain why a World Bank executive could argue that
Africa was "under-polluted." It is all too clear that beyond the African
continent's natural resources, these agencies placed little value on the
continent in general or on the African body in particular.

A particularly egregious example of the ways a corporation can
devalue the bodies of Black women and Black infants is the case of
Nestlé, a food- and drink-processing corporation headquartered in
Switzerland, and its promotion of infant formula throughout continental Africa, where the use of formula has been associated with an
increase in infant mortality.[52] Since the 1930s, nutritionists and health
care professionals have historically railed against corporations that
marketed and sold infant formula to developing countries. Nutrition-

ist Marion Nestle quotes Dr. D. B. Jellifee, a pediatrician, who framed
this as a *moral* issue: "Is it ethical to advertise, using modern techniques
of motivation and persuasion, infant foods in a population that has
no chance financially or hygienically of being able to use them in adequate quantities?"[53] Black women, given their race, class status, and
gender, have borne the brunt of social injustice throughout the era
of coloniality.[54] As such, this case is particularly illustrative because it
is a clear example of how corporations leverage the triple oppression
of gender, race, and class of Black women for corporate profits. Additionally, it is also an example of how Black women chose to stand
in solidarity with and support one another and develop ways to resist
corporate manipulation.

The Nestlé corporation chose to focus on profits rather than the
well-being of its consumers, and the history of racism within the food
and agriculture industry leaves no doubt that the fact that Nestlé's consumers were Black women influenced its decision. According to Marion
Nestle, as late as 1977, Nestlé held 49 percent of the international
formula market, most of which was in developing countries within
continental Africa. A typical infant formula advertisement showed
pictures of Black women nursing their babies with statements such as
"Breast-feed your baby, but when your baby needs a supplement, use
our brand of powdered milk."[55]

In 1981 the World Health Organization and the United Nations
Children's Fund drafted the International Code of Marketing Breast-
Milk Substitutes (the Code). Initially, Nestlé attempted to undermine
the Code and continue marketing its infant formula as it deemed appropriate, and it was not until 1984 that Nestlé finally agreed to adhere
to the Code.[56] It should come as no surprise that after this agreement,
Nestlé began marketing formula and supplements to "pregnant women
in developing countries through advertisements just as misleading as
those that had targeted mothers with infants ('What's good for mom . . .
is better for baby')."[57] Nestlé's actions ought to be seen as particularly
evil, given the cultural significance of motherhood in many African
cultures. Public health scholar Collins O. Airhihenbuwa argues that in
Africa motherhood rather than gender or sexuality is the agency that
matters to a woman's identity.[58] Given this, Airhihenbuwa writes that
African women have responded to the infant formula crisis by reinforc-

ing the communal mothering norms that were already present within their respective cultures. Older mothers are teaching younger mothers how to breastfeed, and collectively they are weighing the benefits and burdens of breastfeeding versus feeding using infant formula, particularly for women whose wage labor or health (i.e., HIV, etc.) makes breastfeeding more challenging.

THE COLOR OF HUNGER

Communities of color feel environmental racism through not only the *placement* of incinerators and landfills but also the *displacement* of accessible vital goods and services. Mark Winne, former executive director of the Hartford Food System, in Hartford, Connecticut, argues that the combination of white flight, low-income households, and urban blight caused many grocery stores to abandon the inner city. Before becoming a national spokesperson for food justice, Winne began his career with the Hartford Food System in 1979. Just ten years earlier, Hartford had thirteen large chain supermarkets within the city limits. By the time Winne arrived in the city in 1979, only six stores remained open, and then by 1986 only two.[59] As he began to research the problem, he discovered that the supermarkets had begun to leave the city after the civil uprisings of 1969—in fact, they followed the exodus of middle- and upper-class whites to the suburbs. These data follow the trend identified by the University of Connecticut's food policy council: grocery stores are fleeing low-income, predominantly Black and Latinx urban areas. Given that 80 percent of Americans buy most of their food in full-size supermarkets, most of which are large chain markets, this flight poses a severe problem regarding food access in urban communities.

Urban areas that lack food markets or access to food markets have been labeled food deserts. These food deserts are found in the most impoverished communities across America—mostly urban areas populated by people of color. However, a more appropriate term that takes coloniality and the structural racism of our food system into account would be food apartheid rather than food desert. A desert is a naturally occurring environmental phenomenon, and there is nothing natural about the strategic displacement of goods that limits Black and other people of color's access to food. As such, food apartheid is a decolonial term inasmuch as it makes explicit the multiple factors that shape our food system: race, income, transportation, location, and access to land, among others.

Food apartheid in urban, predominantly Black and Latinx communities has contributed to what Winne describes as the "food gap." Winne defines the food gap in terms of a "failure of our market economy to serve the basic human needs of those who are impoverished." From a food justice perspective, the food gap is a significant problem facing low-income, inner-city, and rural communities in their struggles to eliminate hunger and food insecurity. Hunger, defined as "the painful sensation that someone feels on a regular basis due to lack of food," is a relatively rare occurrence in the United States today, according to Winne. Unfortunately, however, food insufficiency and food insecurity are much more common: USDA survey data reveal that, on average, between 10 and 12 percent of the US population has low food security, and 3 to 4 percent can be labeled as having very low food security.[60]

Not surprisingly, hunger and poverty are dynamically connected, and they often present us with the age-old "chicken or the egg" question: Which one came first? While it is difficult to definitively say which one causes the other, it is obvious that both poverty and hunger disproportionately affect Black people living in the United States. Bread for the World Institute, an ecumenical Christian agency with the goal of ending world hunger, conducted a survey in 2011 that uncovered startling data to this end. In the United States alone, 27.2 percent of African Americans and 35.7 percent of African American children live below the poverty line compared to 14.5 percent and 19.9 percent of the general population, respectively.[61] Before the 2008 economic recession, African Americans were suffering from higher rates of unemployment and job security than non-Blacks; thus, the 2008 recession exacerbated an already challenging issue for the Black community.

Because poverty and hunger are intimately related, how the United States has dealt with poverty affects our ability to eliminate hunger. Because Americans claim to be an up-by-the-bootstraps kind of people, it has been difficult to sustain support for social welfare programs that are designed to eliminate poverty. Personal responsibility is the argument that many political conservatives (and some liberals behind closed doors) use when speaking about poverty. However, if we recall Du Bois's "tiny community" in rural Tennessee at the beginning of this chapter, it becomes clear that the systematic denial of civil rights has had long-lasting effects on the African American community, one of which is generational poverty, which I am all too familiar with.

Recall that my maternal grandfather, Robert, grew up in a community similar to the one in rural Tennessee described by Du Bois. And while my grandfather was able to move his family from being impoverished to working class, for many years my mother struggled to maintain a working-class wage. This was due in part to the fact that for several years she was a single mother, and we were a single-income household. I am the oldest of four children who grew up in a low-income family, so the twin realities of hunger and poverty are never too far from my thinking. My mother did what most working poor people do: she hustled by working two or three part-time jobs at a time to ensure our family's survival. It is difficult to find suitable words to describe how hard my mother had to work so that we could afford to be poor rather than impoverished. It was relentless love for her children, belief that eventually things would improve, and resilience that motivated her to keep going. In order to ensure that we had enough food to eat, during especially lean times she would purchase food stamps from junkies who wanted to exchange the stamps for cash.[62] If my mother had not worked around the "system" in this and other ways, our family would have had even less to eat. Yet, despite her best efforts, there were times when we did not have enough food in the house, and some of us would go to bed hungry.

GUMBO

In writing this analysis, I have sought to give voice to those whom domestic and international agricultural policy too often ignores: Black people, farmers of color, and poor people. Because much of our agricultural policy exploits the African continent, I wanted the third dish on our vegan soulfull table to remind us of the culinary creativity of the Africans who survived brutal exploitation. This vegan gumbo is an homage to the dark leafy green and soupy stews diet of my West African ancestors. In fact, the English word "okra," a standard item in gumbo recipes, is derived from the Igbo language of Nigeria, where the plant is called *okuru*.[63]

To be sure, policy-makers are not the only ones who tend to ignore all the labor and the laborers who make it possible for us to eat; most of us are, unfortunately, guilty of doing the same. To be fair, this is how industrial food systems are designed to operate: *we consumers are not supposed to think about where our food comes from.* We are supposed to marvel at the multitude of options we have when we're deciding what to eat. We are not supposed to question the environmental sustainability of being able to consume out-of-season produce; instead, we are supposed to eat our strawberries in the winter and be grateful for the miracle of industrial agriculture.

Farmworkers and food workers are supposed to be invisible for most of us who live in the United States, out of sight and out of mind. Charlie LeDuff, the author of the slaughterhouse article that appeared in 2000, has been one of the few journalists able to penetrate a factory farm and give us a glimpse of a world utterly foreign to most of us. The conditions those workers endured just to make ends meet should help us understand why it is so crucial for us to develop ways of purchasing food that delink us from these dehumanizing institutions.

Of the thirty new employees that were hired at the pig slaughter-house with LeDuff, *all the Black women were assigned to the chitterlings room,* where they would scrape worms and feces from pig intestines. Mercedes and Armando Fernández were immigrants from Mexico who were working at the factory to save money so they could move back to Mexico and start a business, but they owed thousands of dollars to the coyote (smuggler) who brought them over the border. Mercedes and her husband felt trapped because they were. Wade Baker, a fifty-one-year-old Black man who grew up during Jim Crow, lamented that while things were better socially for Black people, the ideals of community had seemingly been eaten away by a stagnant economy, promoting an American individualism in which everyone fends for themselves.

During the spring of 2020 the Covid-19 pandemic exacerbated the mistreatment of workers and revealed just how the dehumanizing logics of coloniality are deeply entrenched in the factory farm system. A chilling example took place at a Tyson Foods plant in Waterloo, Iowa, where seven supervisors were fired for allegedly organizing a "cash buy-in, winner-take-all betting pool for supervisors and managers to wager how many employees would test positive for COVID-19."[64] When employees began to become nervous about coming to work and contracting the virus, these same supervisors denied that the virus was spreading at their plant even while they actively avoided going to the plant floor. More than a thousand workers at the plant became infected with the virus, and six employees died, not to mention the countless community members who were infected due to their carelessness. Similar to those at the pig slaughterhouse in North Carolina, many of the plant's employees are immigrants and refugees. For these managers and companies such as Tyson Foods, hiring from these marginalized communities almost ensures that their workforce would be less inclined to risk complaining for fear of losing their job, even if it cost them or their loved ones their life.

Paying attention to these stories allows us to try to understand empathically the suffering underneath these emotions. What are the fears, longings, aching wounds, and gifts that are stifled by working in these dehumanizing conditions? What must it feel like to witness hundreds of deaths every day, being covered in the blood of a nonhuman animal that fought for its life until the bitter end? Imagining ourselves having to work in these conditions, fearing for our livelihood or our lives, should move us to tears and ultimately toward the pursuit of dignity and justice for these workers.

Beyond exposing us to the plight of farm and food workers, this analysis seeks to shed light on two assumptions that shape our current global food system. First, the idea that Black folks were meant to till the land and never acquire the social and political power of landownership is still evident in the treatment of Black farmers and food workers in the United States. The various organizations that wield power within our food system view Black people through racist and colonial ideologies and believe us to be too ignorant to maximize the productive properties of the land through industrial farming. This is unsurprising, given the ways the racist white racial imagination has permeated European American beliefs regarding Black people, agriculture, and food.

The second assumption emerges from the first: corporations exert immense control and influence within our food system, and this has been to the detriment of consumers, farm and food workers, and, as I will describe in chapter 4, the environment. The false beliefs that agribusiness could eliminate farm subsidies and that industrialized farming is the only (or most efficient) way to feed a growing population have helped embed this assumption in both the domestic and global food systems.

So how might we begin thinking through the decolonization of our food systems, both domestic and global? First, we identify the areas where we see coloniality operating in the systems as they are presently constructed: the economic exploitation of farmworkers, food workers, Black farmers and other farmers of color; the dehumanizing working conditions of farm and food workers; poor, rural, and predominantly Black and Latinx communities suffering from food apartheid; and structural racism within the USDA and WTO. Second, we begin to explore and create alternative models from which we can feed ourselves and our communities.

Decolonization asks us to delink from our current food systems and create "food institutions" that are at the service of life. *The current methods of agricultural production, distribution, and consumption operate precisely how they were designed to operate: they prioritize the needs of an elite minority of people at the expense of the global majority and the environment.* This goal begs for the creation of food sovereign communities so that we can ensure food justice for Black and other marginalized communities. Food sovereignty is a community's right to "healthy and culturally appropriate food produced through ecologically sound and sustainable methods, and their right to define their own food and agricultural systems."[65] Conceptually, food sovereignty proposes democratic control over food, from production and processing to distribution, marketing, and consumption. Precisely what role might Christians and religious communities play in the creation of food sovereign communities? Before determining what Christians should do, we must first cultivate the theological ground upon which our ethical commitments will emerge; this is the subject of the next chapter.[66]

Ingredients

coarse sea salt
1 pound chopped collard greens
1 pound chopped mustard greens
½ pound chopped kale
1½ pounds chopped spinach
½ cup extra virgin olive oil
7 garlic cloves, minced
½ cup whole wheat pastry flour
2 large yellow onions, diced
2 large red bell peppers, diced
2 celery ribs, halved lengthwise and chopped
¼ teaspoon cayenne
6 cups vegetable stock
1–2 cups chopped okra
1 tablespoon minced fresh thyme
1 teaspoon filé
1 tablespoon apple cider vinegar
2 green onions, sliced thinly for garnish
2 cups cooked rice

Directions

In a large pot over high heat, bring 4 quarts of water to a boil and add 1 tablespoon of salt. Add all the leafy greens to the water, bring back to a boil, and cook uncovered for 3–4 minutes. Drain in a colander and cool. Transfer the greens to a cutting board and chop well. Combine ¼ cup of the olive oil with the garlic in a large sauté pan until fragrant and starting to turn golden, about 2 minutes. Add the greens mixture, raise the heat to high, sprinkle with 1 teaspoon of salt, and sauté, stirring occasionally, for 2 to 3 minutes, until well coated with oil. Set aside. In a large pot over the lowest heat possible, combine the flour and the remaining olive oil and cook, stirring often with a wooden spoon until caramel colored, about 25 minutes. Add the onion, bell peppers, celery, cayenne, and ½ teaspoon salt. Raise the heat to medium and sauté, stirring occasionally and scraping the bottom of the pot, until the vegetables soften, about 15 minutes. Slowly stir in the stock. Add the reserved greens, bring to a boil, and reduce heat to low. Cover and simmer until the vegetables are tender, about 40 minutes. Stir in the okra and thyme and simmer for an additional 7 minutes. Remove from heat, stir in the filé and apple cider vinegar, and set aside to cool for 10 minutes. Serve garnished with green onions over a bed of rice. The recipe makes 4–6 servings.

Chapter 3
Being Human as Praxis

> The master's minister would occasionally hold services
> for the slaves. . . . Always the white minister used as
> his text something from Paul. At least three or four
> times a year he used as a text: "Slaves, be obedient to
> them that are your masters . . . as unto Christ." Then
> he would go on to show how it was God's will that we
> were slaves and how, if we were good and happy slaves,
> God would bless us. I promised my Maker that if I ever
> learned to read and if freedom ever came, I would not
> read that part of the Bible.
> —Howard Thurman, *Jesus and the Disinherited*

Howard Thurman was born in 1899 in Daytona Beach, Florida. Thurman's maternal grandmother, who was born a slave and lived on a plantation in Florida until emancipation, profoundly influenced his interpretation of Christianity. Her Christian faith played a significant role in guiding Thurman's quest to discern the value of religion to those "with their backs against the wall."[1] Like many slaves, she was a Christian, but since she was unable to read or write, one of Thurman's chores was to read the Bible to her several times per week. Unsurprisingly, Thurman's grandmother was very particular about which texts she wanted him to read and which ones she wanted him to avoid; he was specifically prohibited from reading anything from the Pauline corpus except 1 Corinthians 13.

It was not until Thurman became a young adult that he asked his grandmother why he was never allowed to read the Pauline epistles, and she explained to him how her enslavers had used passages from the Pauline corpus to theologically justify her enslavement. Interpreting the Bible through the lens of coloniality empowered white Christians to manipulate the Gospel of Jesus in ways that seem obviously antithetical to the core of Jesus's spiritual path: the love of God, neighbor, and self. Chattel enslavement seems a clear violation of the command to love your neighbor, *unless* your definition of neighbor is hierarchical, such that folks who do not look, think, and live as you do are viewed as less human. Since the onset of coloniality, neighbor or "human" has become a projection of the fantastic white hegemonic imagination, rendering "human" virtually synonymous with "white men." Thus, the theological problem that has limited the development of an intersectional ecological ethic for Christians has been the (often unconscious) adoption of a way of being human that is filtered through the projection of the white imagination: a racist, sexist, and antiecological way of *practicing being human* that justifies the exploitation of God's Creation: nonhuman nature, human beings, and nonhuman animals.[2]

Limiting the command of neighborly love to prioritize those who perform patriarchal whiteness has had grave consequences for Black, Indigenous, other people of color, and our planet. Delinking what we understand "human" to be from whiteness and maleness is among the most significant projects of decolonial Christian theoethics, and it is also one of the most difficult. If we aim to discover the value of Christian theological ethics for food and environmental justice, we must first decolonize the grounding from which our ethics are derived, the human encounter with God, or theological anthropology.

Borrowing from liberation theologian Dwight Hopkins, I describe theological anthropology as the God-human encounter, because Christians learn both their identity and their purpose as their encounters with the Sacred unfold.[3] As such, *decolonizing Western Christianity's assumptions of the human requires us to view "being human" as praxis, a process of learning, unlearning, applying, and realizing our humanness in antioppressive ways.* For Christians, when being human is understood as praxis, what one looks like becomes unimportant. Rather, our humanness is reflected in our commitment to living in ways that undo the structures of coloniality. The praxis of being human asks us to commit to following Jesus's third way of being in the world and to resist evil with nonviolent compassionate actions rooted in justice, solidarity, and accountability. A sustainable commitment to resisting structural evil places a demand on our spirit that requires us to be—as the ancestral saying goes—grounded in who we are and whose we are. We must avoid falling victim to the lie that our humanness is dependent upon our ability to project white social, cultural, and religious norms.

In his autobiography, Thurman shares how his grandmother helped him and his two siblings remain grounded in who they were and, as importantly, who they were not:

> Once or twice a year, the slave master would permit a slave preacher from a neighboring plantation to come over to preach to his slaves. The slave preacher followed a long tradition . . . to bring the sermon to a grand climax by a dramatization of the crucifixion and resurrection of Jesus. . . . When the slave preacher told the Calvary narrative to my grandmother and the other slaves, it had the same effect on them as it would later have on their descendants. But this preacher, when he had finished, would pause, his eyes scrutinizing every face in the congregation, and then he would tell them, *"You are not n*****s! You are not slaves! You are God's children!"* When my grandmother got to that part of her story, there would be a slight stiffening in her spine as we sucked in our breath. When she had finished, our spirits were restored.[4]

The theological and psychological work of decolonizing the human person, committing ourselves to being human in ways that undo the structures of coloniality, can be overwhelming unless we remember, rest in, and are grounded in the fact that we too are children of the living God. When grounded in the truth of who we are, we are empowered by the sustaining presence of God's love to resist structural evil in its multivalent forms.

For Black Christians, prioritizing food and environmental justice is critical, because we bear the disproportionate burden of ecological harm. As an act of justice, Black Christians and those committed to the liberation of marginalized folk should develop foodways that contribute to the flourishing of Black and other marginalized communities. In this way, the motivation for food and environmental justice emerges from our moral obligation of exercising care for the human person, for our communities, and especially for marginalized peoples and their environments. To be sure, some may see my suggestion that prioritizing the care of human persons is in alignment with caring for the environment as problematic and liable to anthropocentrism. However, this anthropocentric critique is grounded in an understanding of environmentalism that emerges from a dualistic notion of the human. The claim that human beings exist apart from nature, a claim steeped in white supremacist thinking, is precisely what a decolonial theological anthropology aims to correct. Human beings live within environments teeming with life, and prioritizing human welfare, especially the welfare of marginalized life, does not have to be at odds with developing sustainable ecologies.

The third step in decolonizing soul food attends to being. Given the knowledge we have gained about the Black agricultural and culinary past and the social conditions that we presently find our communities within, how might we practice being human in ways that enable us to heal from the psychological terror of colonial thinking? How might a renewed understanding of what it means to practice being human shape the development of antioppressive foodways and agricultural practices? The aim of this chapter is to answer those questions by constructing a decolonial theological anthropology for Christians that countervails the tacit but dominant understanding of the human person that places whiteness and maleness as pinnacles of Creation. The theological anthropology outlined here attempts to equip Christians with the necessary theological scaffolding to reimagine the God-human encounter through a renewed understanding of self-love, solidarity, and holistic interdependence. These three principles serve as guideposts for the development of decolonial foodways, agricultural practices, and socioeconomic commitments that aim to attend to the immediate suffering of Black communities and promote the long-term flourishing of those selfsame communities.

THE INVENTION OF "MAN" AND WESTERN THEOLOGICAL ANTHROPOLOGY

In their book *The History of the World in Seven Cheap Things*, Raj Patel and Jason Moore offer a compelling portrait of our modern world and helpfully identify some of the thinkers and ideas that still influence how we make meaning out of our existence. Of the seven "cheap" things they identify, two of them are useful for analyzing the theological anthropology of Western Christianity: cheap nonhuman nature and cheap human and nonhuman lives.

By cheap, the authors do not mean that nature and lives are economically cheap, though that is a part of their argument. They understand the cheapening of nature and lives as a "strategy, a practice, a violence that mobilizes all kinds of work—human and animal, botanical and geological—with as little compensation as possible."[5] *Something can be cheapened once we create relational distance from it.* Moreover, our distance from "it" allows us to make it into an object. We cheapen it by making it into a "thing," essentially, a nonsentient object. It is our inability to recognize and accept our relational responsibilities as a part of nature that enables human beings to cheapen subjects into objects.

While cheapening life clearly has an economic dimension, I do not agree with the authors' conclusions that the cheapening of nature and life can be attributed solely to capitalism, though capitalism plays an important role. Instead, I suggest that capitalism as a structural economic system is a symptom of a deeper malady that plagues the ideological foundations of modern Western thinking about what counts as life and whose lives actually count. Indeed, coloniality is the foundation upon which the logic of cheapening is built.

Coloniality as a way of thinking emerged during the sixteenth-century European encounters with the Indigenous peoples of what would later become the Americas. These encounters mark the beginnings of European American empires that played the primary role in ushering us into our current global ecological crisis. Empire making of this magnitude has historically required the cheapening of life (human and nonhuman animal, poor, women) for the benefit of those elite few in power. To be sure, empire making was not new. Coloniality is what sets European American empires apart from others. The logic of coloniality enabled nonhuman life and certain human bodies (Black, brown, poor, and female) to be policed in new ways that would render them perpetually cheap by placing them within dualistic hierarchies, particularly the hierarchies of society and nature.

Our modern understanding of the word "society" is a product of colonial thinking: "Beginning in the middle of the 16th century, society came to mean not just the company that we keep, but also a bigger whole of which individuals are a part."[6] Human beings have seemingly always given names to establish boundaries between social groups: Christendom, Sunni or Shia, the Middle Kingdom, among others. But our modern notion of society has a historically unique antonym: nature. One is either a part of society or a part of nature. You are either a human fit for society, or you are a savage who must be developed out of savagery, eliminated for the sake of modernization and development, or abandoned to environmental spaces believed to be of little value to society.

Once nature and society take upon these new distinctions, they allow for a new way of organizing and structuring human encounters with the earth that enables certain lives to be cheapened and rendered merely as things. The artificial boundary between society and nature created the relational distance necessary for nonwhite and nonhuman lives to be cheapened. Indeed, the hierarchical logic of coloniality made policing the alleged boundary between society and nature essential if the modern conception of nature was to flourish and take hold in the consciousness of European colonialists.

Philosophers and scientists such as René Descartes and Francis Bacon played vital roles in establishing such boundaries. Descartes's dualistic distinction between the reality of the mind (*res cogitans*) and the materiality of the body (*res extensa*), between "thinking things" and "extended things," became one method by which boundaries were policed. Human beings were thinking things, and extended things existed in nature. However, not all human beings were viewed as thinking things. The privilege of being viewed as a thinking thing was only bestowed upon European men, and according to Descartes, it was they who must become the "masters and possessors of nature."[7]

The lineage of Descartes's thinking can be traced back a generation earlier, when Francis Bacon was among those ushering the West into a scientific revolution. Bacon, who at different times was a member of Parliament and the attorney general of England and Wales, argued that "science should, as it were, torture nature's secrets out of her. And further that the 'empire of man' should penetrate and dominate the womb of nature."[8] The invention of the dualistic binaries of nature/ society was profoundly and purposefully gendered to reify the human, the European man. In this way, Baconian scientific theory and Cartesian dualism are much more than a part of the foundation of modern science and philosophy. They are normative descriptions of how we are told to best understand or organize power and hierarchy: human beings above nature, men above women, Europeans above all nonwhites, colonizer over colonized.

The hierarchical ordering of bodies was not a new concept to those responsible for the emergence of the European American empires and colonial dominance. Hierarchies had existed in the West for some time. However, during the fifteenth and sixteenth centuries, ideas begin to circulate that enabled the nation-state and Christian theology to weaponize hierarchy in order to cheapen human life. With regard to statecraft, John Locke emerges as a central figure whose writings helped concretize the legal cheapening of human life in the United States. In his *Second Treatise of Government,* he writes that "the fundamental constitutions affirm that every freeman of Carolina shall have absolute power and authority over his Negro slaves."[9] What's frightening is that Locke ensured that the words "power and" would precede "authority," thus affirming the nation-state's power to condemn Black and brown bodies to the status of chattel. It's worth noting that Locke is the same person who would go on to write that "every man has a property in his own person." While some have tried to suggest that this contradiction points to a change in Locke's thinking during his later years, a more compelling and accurate argument is that Locke's thinking regarding Black slaves relative to the state was consistent with the thinking of Anthony Ashley Cooper, 1st Earl of Shaftesbury, Locke's economic patron, who had a vested economic interest in the enslavement of Indigenous and African bodies.

While the nation-state's interest in weaponizing the concept of racial and gender hierarchy was primarily economic, for the Roman Catholic and Protestant Churches, the interest seemed to align with a desire for their ways of practicing Christianity to conform to nationalist empire-making ideologies. During the early stages of European colonialism, Prince Henry the Navigator and Christopher Columbus become central figures in defining the European *Christian* man as the human ideal and non-European human beings as Others. In the wake of his voyage around the southern tip of Africa, Prince Henry claimed that Europeans were culturally and religiously superior to Africans. Henry asserted that the African cultural and religious practices were demonic, made aesthetic judgments based on Africans' skin color, and inaugurated the transatlantic slave trade based upon those judgments.[10] He was crucial to the racial and theological production of the human when we consider the role that religion, culture, and eventually skin color played in justifying the enslavement of Africans. Columbus built upon the work of Prince Henry by applying the same concepts to the Indigenous peoples of North and South America. Carter notes that Columbus's logs describe the newly "discovered" lands as *terra nullius* (lands of no one) and their inhabitants as less than or insufficiently human due to their physical appearance and cultural and religious practices, which deviated from Eurocentric norms. Moreover, he gave the islands "such names as 'the Holy Trinity' (Trinidad) and 'St. Mary of the Holy Conception' (the Virgin Islands)," even further embedding the story of his discoveries within the context of the Genesis Creation narratives and Christian eschatology.[11]

By understanding and contextualizing his imperial mission through a theological lens, Columbus created the framework necessary for Christian European white men to view themselves as imperial God-men. Theologically, European American Christians openly wondered if Africans and Indigenous Americans bore the imprint of the *imago Dei?* Were they created in the image of God, as all humans are understood to be, based on the Genesis Creation narratives? And if so, did they reflect the image of God to the same degree as European men? By suggesting that Black, Indigenous, and other nonwhite bodies were not quite as human as European bodies were, European Christian men felt no moral obligation to treat enslaved Africans as they would other human beings.

It is no coincidence, then, that colonialism and chattel slavery emerged during the period when European Christian men were able to claim that Africans and Indigenous American people were evil and savage because they were either non-Christian or "too close to nature" and "like animals" and therefore distant from God. For the church, hierarchy is weaponized as a way to theoethically justify the immoral and unjust cheapening of life by European American people in general and men in particular. In so doing, religious orders sought to normalize the oppression experienced by marginalized folks as either divinely ordained or worthy of reward in the afterlife. To be sure, Thurman correctly identified the theological consequences of normalizing white racism toward people of color when he wrote that if the attitude is viewed as normal, then it is correct; if correct, then moral; if moral, then religious.[12]

By fashioning their theological anthropology through the lens of coloniality and white dominance, predominantly white Christian churches (Roman Catholic, mainline, and nondenominational) and religious leaders have been able to weaponize the cheapening of non-white human life in ways that have enabled them to maintain political power that is tied to empire. One needs to look no further than the white evangelical Christians and their religious leaders and their high approval rating of Donald Trump. Despite Trump's mishandling of the Covid-19 pandemic, racist anti-immigration and anti-asylum-seeking policies, health care policies that disproportionately harm people of color and poor people, and inability to articulate basic Christian norms such as loving one's neighbor, a poll conducted in April 2020 revealed that 56 percent of white Christians approve of the way Trump handled his job as president. A closer examination of the poll shows just how significant a factor race is in framing one's approval or disapproval of Trump; 72 percent of white evangelical Protestants (compared to just 12 percent of Black Protestants) and 54 percent of white Roman Catholics (compared to 23 percent of Hispanic Catholics) steadfastly supported him.[13] The racial divide in these polls speaks volumes; white American Christians tend to interpret what it means to be human and practice Christianity in ways that normalize the dehumanization and suffering of people of color. Indeed, the modern understanding of what it means to be human, to be an "Anthropos," is an event grounded in the white hegemonic imagination and supported by Western white Christian norms and ideologies. As such, slavery, colonialism, segregation, and the logic of capitalist development that emerged from colonialism can all be understood as a problem of a particular white Western Christian theological anthropology.

US THEOLOGICAL ANTHROPOLOGY
AND AFRICAN AMERICANS

The theological anthropology that emerged in concert with coloniality, which defined Black and other nonwhite bodies as Others and has helped to facilitate the othering rationale to nonhuman nature itself, is still the dominant way of interpreting humanness within US Christian culture. This view of the human person limits the ability of all life (human or otherwise) to flourish by prioritizing the needs of a proportionally small segment of white men over the needs of the rest of our ecosystem.

As it relates to Black people, this understanding of the human person is particularly oppressive because it reinforces theological and anthropological claims about Black bodies that have historically undermined our struggle against coloniality and anti-Black racism. This framework dehumanized Africans and other non-European people and projected the idea that they were better suited as beasts of burden fit only for service and slavery. The animalization and concomitant dehumanization of Africans were critical in order to theologically and ideologically justify the mistreatment of African slaves. In viewing Africans as not fully human, slave owners and proponents of chattel slavery could claim that enslavement was not immoral and arguably in the best interest of the enslaved. As noted in the story of Thurman's grandmother, some European colonists and slaveholders even argued that there were evangelistic merits to conquest and enslavement; after all, at least the "savages" could find freedom in heaven through Christianity.

The theological beliefs about nonwhite bodies enabled European American Christians to accept anthropological claims that justified their theological norms. From the fantastic white imagination of anthropologists from the eighteenth through the early twentieth century, the notion that Africans and other non-European people were less human was concretized through the misinterpretation of Darwin's theory of evolution. Social Darwinism is an ideology that interprets the oppression of different races, classes, and species as a rationally justified demonstration of evolution in action. In this way, Darwin's theory of evolution as the "survival of the fittest" was appropriated by racist white anthropologists for their own use in a theory of winners and losers in social history.

Social Darwinists argued that "fitness" was genetic; therefore, those who were fit passed their fit genes on to their children, while the unfit did likewise. Animal activist Marjorie Spiegel notes that as late as the 1960s "charts depicting the evolution of primates from distant ancestors, up through various hominids, to a Black person, and finally to a fully upright Aryan male" were still present within the scientific community.[14] Given the racial hierarchy that was already present in the United States, social Darwinism should also be understood as a scientific means of justifying the racism against and the oppression of Blacks and other people of color.

Proponents of social Darwinism enabled the anthropologically justified notion that Black people were somehow less than human to persist unchecked in the collective conscience of America. Within the field of medicine, the animalization of Blacks enabled doctors to justify the use of Black people's bodies in experimental research. Emilie Townes has described several of these experiments in her work on African American health care and has argued that many of the false ideas about Blacks' biological differences and disease susceptibility created by these experiments still linger within black and European American communities today.

Perhaps the most well-known scientific experiment on Black bodies was the Tuskegee syphilis study, which was conducted from 1932 to 1972 by the US Public Health Service and involved four hundred Black men who were neither told that they had syphilis nor treated for it once doctors discovered that penicillin cured the disease.[15] The purpose of the study was to observe the men as they died and autopsy them to study the damage that untreated syphilis rendered to their internal organs. Townes argues that the genesis of this experiment began in the early 1900s with the development of the "syphilitic Negro concept." During this period, the diagnosis of syphilis centered on the variety and size of lesions the disease produced. This meant that dermatologists played a primary role in diagnosing the disease and opened the door for racial interpretations (i.e., differences in "skin") to flourish within the medical community. One New York physician, Howard Fox, wrote that syphilis and several other diseases were more likely to affect Black people due to the "dermatological peculiarities of the negro."[16]

Unsurprisingly, medical professionals rarely considered the role of the environment in affecting the health of Black people. Instead of accounting for living conditions, physicians believed that Blacks had higher incidences of pneumonia and tuberculosis because they had smaller lungs than whites. Physicians also believed that "Black skin, big glands, big livers, and big kidneys"—all of which they thought Black people possessed—allowed Blacks to "throw off heat" and better endure hot working conditions. Moreover, they believed that the "small hearts and brains" of Blacks accounted for their "childlike behavior and absolute dependence on whites."[17] Indeed, this "scientific" view of Black people as dull and dumb resonates with the racialized food ideologies I describe in chapter 1. Whether it is in science or popular culture, Americans were and still are being fed the message that Black people are genetically and culturally inferior to whites.

When we consider how embedded the US racial project is within the economic, political, and ideological structure of America, we should not be surprised that Black people would interpret this worldview simultaneously as both suspect and normative. While racism disguised as Christian practice has historically been something Black Christians have critiqued, I suggest that we have not sufficiently attended to the assumptions within normative Western theological anthropology that support the ideology of Black people as less human than whites. Rather than deconstructing and refashioning what it means to be human in light of our critique of white colonial Christianity, Black theologians and religious leaders historically have argued that we are just as "human" as white people are. What I am suggesting is that the racist, sexist, and androcentric definition of the human, which emerged during the era of coloniality, is incompatible with the religion of Jesus—as such, being just as human as white people does little to deconstruct racism, sexism, and the ecological extractivist thinking that normalizes oppression.

In an open letter written to an incarcerated Angela Davis, the essayist and social critic James Baldwin describes with poignant clarity the psychological and emotional impact of US theological anthropology on Black people in America:

The American triumph—in which the American tragedy has always been implicit—was to make black people despise themselves. When I was little I despised myself, I did not know any better. And this meant, albeit unconsciously, or against my will, or in great pain, that I also despised my father. And my mother. And my brothers. And my sisters. Black people were killing each other every Saturday night out on Lenox Avenue, when I was growing up; and no one explained to them, or to me, that it was intended that they should; that they were penned where they were, like animals, in order that they should consider themselves no better than animals. Everything supported this sense of reality, nothing denied it: and so one was ready, when it came time to go to work, to be treated as a slave. So one was ready, when human terrors came, to bow before a white God and beg Jesus for salvation.[18]

Here Baldwin hints at how some Christian norms encouraged Black people to seek freedom from oppression through eschatological salvation rather than seeking freedom through the elimination of the oppressive structures themselves. Most importantly, Baldwin gestures toward the relationship between *racism* and *animalization,* a relationship that is foundational to the normalization of Black exploitation and oppression.

RACE, RELIGION, AND THE CREATION OF "THE ANIMAL"

Most Christian activists and theologians of color who do antiracist or human rights work have touched upon "the animal question" in some way. A thorough analysis of racism or coloniality usually calls attention to the degree to which racialized folks are animalized or referenced as behaving "like animals."[19] That is, those who seek to maintain (or create) an oppressive dynamic between two groups often describe the marginalized group as falling outside of the realm of "human" as a way to legitimize behaviors that would otherwise be considered immoral at best and evil at worst. However, the analysis done by most theologians of color on the relationship between antiracism and animalization tends to stop at this point, followed by the claim that we people of color "are humans too" and should be treated as such rather than being treated "like animals."

I agree with Black feminist Syl Ko's claim that this way of thinking requires "an *open acceptance* of the negative status of 'the animal' which . . . is a *tacit acceptance of the hierarchical racial system of white supremacy in general.*" The human/animal divide, as Western white Christianity constructed it during coloniality, is a part of the theological and ideological foundation that supports the framework of white supremacy. This means that *our modern delineation of human/humanity and animal/animality was constructed along racial lines.* As a result, the negative notion that human beings have of "the animal" is the anchor of the system of white colonial logic and the ideology of white dominance.[20] Psychologist and postcolonial/decolonial theorist Frantz Fanon made this clear in *The Wretched of the Earth* when he wrote: "In plain talk, [the colonial subject] is reduced to the state of an animal. And consequently, when the colonist speaks of the colonized he uses zoological terms. Allusion is made to the slithery movements of the yellow race, the odors from the 'native' quarters. . . . In his endeavors at description and finding the right word, the colonist refers constantly to the bestiary."[21] Antiracist activists have understood these connections for a number of years. What I am suggesting here is that the strategy of claiming Black "humanity" to subvert the theological and anthropological norms that enabled the creation of our white supremacist society will remain ineffective if we do not attend to the human/animal tension as well.

The moral and ideological frameworks that support racism and white supremacy and the frameworks that created our current understanding of "the animal" are deeply intertwined and cannot be adequately addressed independently of one another. As Syl Ko notes, these ideological frameworks "were creations invented by a small percentage of people who took themselves to be the singular point of knowledge and, through centuries of violence, genocide, and control, made their view of the world, themselves, and others universal."[22] As long as the Western white theological anthropology that constructed "the human" and "the animal" as such remains intact, the ideological support for anti-Black racism and white supremacy remains intact.

To be sure, when someone states that a group of human beings is animalistic, they do not mean that the group of people falls outside of the scientific category of *Homo sapiens.* Rather, they are stating that these human beings do not look, live, worship, or reason normally, where "normal" is understood as Eurocentric white male norms. In other words, when one does not *act white* or when one behaves in ways that challenge white dominance and the hierarchy of white supremacy, one is seen as an animal. Depending upon how well some "animals" can replicate the norms that Western white Christian men dictated as human norms, certain nonwhite human-animals could be treated *like* humans, even if they could not really *be* human. In this way, the white racial imagination's conception of "the animal"—developed within a culture of Christian white male supremacy—is the conceptual vehicle that morally and ideologically justifies violence against subhuman (e.g., people of color) and nonhuman (animal) Others.[23]

Put simply, the methodological reasoning that normalizes racism and white supremacy does not discriminate based on species. When nonhuman nature is viewed through the lens of philosopher David Nibert's theory of oppression, it becomes clear that nonhuman nature—particularly the nonhuman animals within it—is entangled within the same oppressive logic that continues to justify racism, violence, and the marginalization of Black and other people of color. Nibert argues that "the arrangements that lead to various forms of oppression are integrated in such a way that the exploitation of one group frequently augments and compounds the mistreatment of others."[24]

To be clear, I am not suggesting that the oppression and exploitation of nonhuman animals are the same as those of human beings. However, I am arguing that the exploitation of nonhuman animals normalizes a colonial theological anthropology—a dualistic and hierarchical understanding of the human person that justifies the exploitation of nonhuman others, where human is understood to mean straight white men and those who perform whiteness as such—which in turn normalizes anti-Black racism.

The three factors of Nibert's theory of oppression can be easily applied to nonhuman animals. The first factor, economic exploitation and competition for resources, is painfully evident in recent human history. The economic value of items such as elephant ivory and rhinoceros horns has pushed these animals to the brink of extinction.[25] Additionally, species such as the gray wolf and the bison were also once hunted to near extinction because they "competed" with colonial settlers for land in the midwestern and western United States.[26] That the second factor, unequal power that is largely vested in control of the state, contributes to animal oppression seems obvious. The gray wolf and the bison did not possess the political power to prevent their near extinction.

The last factor, ideological control, has an unfortunate history within America. Racist ideologies have long contributed to the dehumanization of people of color in this country. Indeed, I have discussed at length how the dehumanization and animalization of Black people justified our oppression in the minds of the oppressors. Likewise, nonhuman animals have suffered by being othered; they too feel the consequences of being viewed as "just animals," lesser beings that humans use for their benefit rather than as intricate components of Creation. Arguably the most egregious example of nonhuman animal othering in the twentieth and twenty-first centuries is the treatment of domestic animals in concentrated animal feeding operations, that is, factory farms. The experience of the Smithfield factory farm workers that I examined in chapter 2 reminds us that nonhuman animals are not the only ones who suffer within these walls; nonhuman animals pay the ultimate price, but each day a little piece of the lives of the workers slips away too.

Nibert's theory helps us understand that unless there is a system in place to prevent exploitation, humans have a history of eliminating or exploiting groups they perceive to be unlike themselves when it economically benefits them to do so. The oppressor must have the power to oppress the members of the minority group, and the oppressor typically exerts this power through political control. As such, the oppressor holds the majority (if not all) of the power within the state and has the ability to create and enforce the law. Finally, social ideologies that have fueled prejudiced attitudes and discriminatory acts are promoted to normalize and maintain oppressive economic and social arrangements.[27] By appearing normal and almost natural, oppressive structures are allowed to maintain an air of invisibility to the populations that enjoy or gain benefit from them. That such treatment of nonhuman animals is justified using the same techniques and logic of exploitation that have been used for centuries on Blacks in America ought to cause all people, but especially Black people, to critically examine how coloniality has influenced our understanding of the human person in ways that might cause us to normalize exploitative relationships within our environments and with nonhuman animals.

To summarize, the core message embedded within colonial Western Christian theological anthropology is that in order to be Christian, one must become "human," and in order to become human, one must become white, and in order to become white, one must accept the hierarchy that protects the image of the heterosexual white male as the image of God on earth, the pinnacle of Creation. By this, I do not mean to say that American Christians have *explicitly* been taught (at least in the post–civil rights era) that being raced as white and interpreting the world through the white racial frame is the ideal. Rather, American Christians are socialized to accept a normative structure of Christianity that places humans at the pinnacle of Creation. The white racial imagination, racial formation, and racism ensure that the human is understood to be white, patriarchy ensures that he is male, and heterosexism ensures that he is straight.

Since the onset of colonialism, Christians, regardless of race, who have striven to be seen as "fully human" have been striving toward a flawed theological principle that replicates an oppressive hierarchal model that places whiteness and maleness as pinnacles of Creation. This is the theological and anthropological problem that currently confronts all Christians but is particularly problematic for Black, Indigenous, and other Christians of color. Unless we attend to this theological anthropology, the majority of Christians (women, people of color, LGBTQ, etc.) and especially Black Christians are at risk of subscribing to the theological norms that have normalized our exploitation and the exploitation of nonhuman nature.

Decolonial thinking asks us to reimagine and redefine the human outside of the framework of coloniality, a framework that purports that the value of a life, including that of our own lives, is determined by how much said life supports institutions that benefit from our exploitation. With respect to food and environmental justice, decolonial thinking requires us to discern how our theological anthropology ought to shape the relationships we have with our communities, including nonhuman animals, if we aim to cultivate a way of being human that resists the exploitative logic of coloniality. One form of oppression cannot be attended to in its totality without attending to the other.

TOWARD A DECOLONIAL THEOLOGICAL ANTHROPOLOGY

How does decolonial thinking help Christians reinterpret the God-human encounter in ways that decenter the colonial person and prioritize our interdependence with human beings and nonhuman nature? First, decolonial thinking recognizes that the epistemological foundation of Western Christianity is entwined within the logic of coloniality and as such seeks to distill knowledge about the human person from the history and practices that gave life to marginalized communities. Given the psychic hold of coloniality, a secondary requirement of developing a decolonial theological anthropology is to take what Thurman describes as an "inward journey" during which we begin to answer the question Who are we, really?, to which I add a second question, Whom do we want to be and become? This critically reflexive soul work enables us to seek out and dismantle the sentinels that have dutifully guarded the colonialist logic that consciously or unconsciously influences our thoughts about the human person, Christian ethics, and food and environmental justice.

The decolonial theological anthropology I construct begins by exploring the Creation narratives to recast the God-human relationship in ways that can lead to the collective flourishing of all creation. To be sure, my hope is that this construction of the human person resonates with all Christians regardless of race. However, if Black bodies, particularly the bodies of Black women, having been cast as the marginalized Others in white American theological anthropology, are free to realize a liberatory selfhood, then freedom for *all* other bodies would follow. As such, my theological anthropology finds its starting point in the theological writings of Black women scholars.[28]

From an ecological perspective and in light of the sociohistorical knowledge we have uncovered in chapters 1 and 2, the decolonial theological anthropology I develop aims to describe who people are called to be, how people are called to live, and what we are called to do in the world. This theological anthropology is informed by decolonial theological themes found within the Genesis Creation narratives and the Gospel stories of Jesus, themes that are consistent with the teachings and wisdom that have sustained and nourished those who have lived with their backs against the wall for far too long. The norm that makes this theological anthropology decolonial is the nonnegotiable theological principle that all creation has sacred worth and that no created being should be exploited in the eyes of God. When applied to our theological anthropology, this norm results in three critical assumptions for a decolonial understanding of the human person.

First, all human beings are created in the image of God and are called to love ourselves—regardless—as womanist thinkers have consistently reminded us. As such, we should view ourselves as a human freed from the white Christian patriarchal norms that created and justified the exploitation of an "Other." Second, human beings should strive to create human-God, human-human, and human-nature relationships that mirror the life and teachings of Jesus, whose earthly ministry was to be in solidarity with those who are marginalized and to care for the others, or the "least of these." Lastly, all life, human and otherwise, is holistically interdependent, and human life cannot flourish independently from other ecological life. Given this, human beings have a divinely appointed vocation to care for the earth, which is a part of carrying out the mission of God.

These three categories—self-love, solidarity, and holistic interdependence—are generative insofar as they enable the construction of a counternarrative that uplifts the dignity, value, and capabilities of bodies gendered as female and raced as Black, Indigenous, or other people of color. In the final sections, I describe how a decolonial interpretation of these three theological categories builds upon and informs them in ways that should be foundational in how we care for ourselves and our broader environments.

CREATION NARRATIVES

My process for fashioning a decolonial theological anthropology begins by reexamining the Creation narratives within the Bible to unearth the vision these early followers of God had in mind for the vocation of being human. This move toward scripture may seem odd for some: Why would I use an ancient text to develop a contemporary decolonial theological understanding of the human person?

First, for Christians, scripture still plays a vital role in informing notions of whom we ought to be and what we ought to do in light of our beliefs in the communities that I work with. The Creation narratives are useful inasmuch as they reflect broader norms that Black communities have come to know as true through our encounters with nonhuman nature and the divine. This fact alone is reason enough for me as a practical theologian to include scripture in my reconstructive project. Second, because these narratives carry the weight of hundreds of years of misinterpretation that helped to reinforce the exploitation of people, nonhuman animals, and our environment, these narratives must be addressed, even if briefly, to discern how they could help shape a new anthropology that resists coloniality in all its forms. Third, I agree with systematic theologian Willie Jennings, who argues that "theorists and theories of race will not touch the ground until they reckon deeply with the foundations of racial imaginings in the deployment of an altered theological vision of creation."[29] European American race thinking delinked human identity from the land and landscapes and tied our understanding of self and our communities to our bodies to promote white bodily power and solidarity among those who understood themselves to be white. Decolonizing ourselves from this broken theological anthropology requires us to reimagine our relationship with nonhuman nature and reinterpret our sacred text in ways that foster a vision of self-love, solidarity, and holistic interconnectedness. In this way, the Creation narratives are generative for decolonial thinking insofar as they decenter the human from whiteness and suggest an intimate interdependence between all created life.

Biblical writers lived within an agricultural economy and were aware of the importance of ecology—particularly agrarianism—in their society. They lived with the keen awareness that proper care of the land was critical for their society to flourish. Reading the Creation narratives from an agrarian perspective enables us to reimagine the God-human relationship through our divinely appointed earth care responsibilities. While a full exegetical analysis of the narratives is not necessary for our purposes, there are three themes that emerge from the narratives that are helpful in developing a decolonial theological anthropology: imagination, the responsibility of care, and the *imago Dei*, the theological doctrine that human beings are created in the image of God.

Theological and secular philosophers alike have accused the first Creation narrative of encouraging an anthropocentric view of nature. If read literally and through the lens of colonial theological anthropology, Genesis 1:28 appears to show God blessing and encouraging humanity to "subdue" and have "dominion" over the earth and other animals: "God blessed them, and God said to them, 'Be fruitful and multiply, and fill the earth and subdue it; and have dominion over the fish of the sea and over the birds of the air and over every living thing that moves upon the earth'" (NRSV).

Following biblical scholars such as Ellen Davis and Walter Brueggemann, I suggest that these stories should be read as poetry designed to inspire a landless community. Reading Genesis 1 as a *liturgical poem* invites us to see Creation through a divine perception that encourages a healthy imagination to think and feel in ways that promote relationality and interdependence.[30] Indeed, viewing it as a poem allows us to take every word seriously, since in good poetry, every word is deliberately chosen. Furthermore, this perspective acknowledges that poems contain a surplus of meaning and therefore have the potential to say something new and meaningful to different audiences at different times. God is still speaking to and through us, and this perspective invites us to read scripture as the word of the *living* God.

Interpreted through a poetic lens, the language of "dominion" and "subdue" connotes a view of the human vocation where human beings are assigned special status and power within a hierarchical worldview. To be sure, the hierarchical view of human beings in relationship to nonhuman nature does not necessarily lead to an oppressive dynamic between human beings and nonhuman nature by default. Instead, it is a theological anthropology guided by coloniality that elevates white heterosexual men as imperial God-men who believe they should have the power to control the natural world that creates an oppressive dynamic between human beings and nonhuman nature. Both the first and second Creation narratives invite us to imagine a world where nonhuman nature and animals are a part of our family because we were all created from the same "stuff," the dust from the fertile soil of the earth. The family is the primary space where we can experience the responsible and loving aspects of hierarchy between grandparents, parents, and children. As such, dominion can be understood as a human position of sacred responsibility of care designated by God and a model for the responsible use and exercise of power.[31] Coloniality has made this perspective of "dominion" difficult to imagine, particularly for many of us academics who are trained—indeed steeped—in a worldview built on the logic of whiteness.

The beauty of Genesis 1 is that it forces us to reimagine a world where human beings strive to live in antioppressive relationships with other created beings because of our relationship *with* the land rather than our domination *over* it. Our kinship with the land is demonstrated in how we maintain our relationship with the land. Writing specifically about the human vocation and the sacred responsibility to care for the land, the writers of Genesis 2:15 state: "The Lord God took the [human] and put him in the Garden of Eden to till it and keep it." Importantly, while the New Revised Standard Version translates the Hebrew verbs as "till" and "keep" and the Tanakh translates them as "till" and "tend," these verbs are the customary terms to express service to another and servitude in general.[32] When we read with both verb meanings in mind, we can read the text as stating that a distinctive part of the human vocation of caring for the earth is to both *keep* and *serve* the garden, to *learn* from it while *respecting* its limitations.

Genesis 2 reveals that humanity's relationship with the land emerges from our natural kinship: "And the Lord God formed the human being [adam], dust from the fertile soil [adama]" (Genesis 2:7, Davis's translation).[33] We are connected to the land and therefore to our environments because we understand ourselves as materializing from the land. The human/nature split that is a product of colonial thinking, a split that still permeates many theologically informed environmental writings by the ways they distinguish between the care of human beings from the care of the "environment," must be abandoned if we are going to take earth care and food justice seriously.

My idea of a responsible and loving hierarchy that emphasizes care and interdependence is informed by my reading of Genesis 1:26: "Let us make humankind in our image, according to our likeness" (NRSV). What is important to note here is that the vocational responsibility of care for our community is given to humans on the basis that human beings are created in the image of God. Historically, the concept of the *imago Dei* had been reserved for royalty in the ancient Near Eastern context; this perspective was clearly incorporated into the colonial definition of the human person. However, the writers of Genesis 1 boldly democratized the concept and thereby made it possible for all of humanity to participate in God's rule on the earth through the communal exercise of antioppressive forms of power.[34]

SELF-LOVE

What does it mean for Black people to be described as imaging God? How does being created in the image of God reshape our attitudes toward other humans, nonhuman nature, and ourselves? I contend that by embracing the biblical claim that we are created in the image of God, Black Christians can break free from the white Christian theological and anthropological norms that designated us as less than human, or human inasmuch as we live in ways that do not challenge white dominance.

Jesus's incarnation as a human being is significant when we consider his embodiment in light of his teaching of the greatest commandment: to love God with all one's heart, soul, and strength and to love one's neighbor as oneself. Womanist theologian Karen Baker-Fletcher contends that to see Jesus as fully human and fully God is to see Jesus as "a manifestation of Spirit in Creation working in harmony with itself."[35] Building upon the Nicene Creed, which states that Jesus is both fully God and fully human, Baker-Fletcher contends that Jesus is both fully spirit and fully dust—fully God and fully connected to all elements that comprise the earth.[36] If we follow Baker-Fletcher's depiction of Jesus as both fully human and fully God, then loving Jesus requires that we must love God, Creation, and human beings, including ourselves. *In this way, the unconditional love of Jesus requires an unconditional love of self.* Moreover, the ability of Black Christians to love ourselves also requires the ability to see the divine reflected, however dimly, within us.

For Black Christians, embracing the divine command to love ourselves is crucial because it allows our communities to begin to heal the psychological residue of coloniality: internalized racism, colorism, dehumanization, and the animalization of our Black bodies. To be sure, self-love is not merely an individual exercise. The pain and anguish of racism and exploitation have been felt by our entire community, and cultivating compassion for our communities and for ourselves involves communal contemplative practices such as communal lament.

Emilie Townes has argued that communal lament can be formative for the Black community because it "names problems, seeks justice, and hopes for God's deliverance." In this way, communal lament enables us to identify the fears, longings, aching wounds, and stifled gifts that have hindered Black people's ability to love ourselves, regardless. Communal lament helps us name the psychological consequences of a colonial theological anthropology so that we might attend to these wounds with compassionate care. Townes notes that when we grieve and lament, "we acknowledge and live the experience rather than try to hold it away from us out of some misguided notion of being objective or strong."[37] Consequently, we can name the theological and anthropological category of "Other" as demonic in order to loosen its grasp on our consciousness so that we can move toward healing.

Healing from the woundedness of othering requires the ability to love oneself; however, Baldwin's words are a testament to the difficulty of this task within our communities. I believe that the ability to see the divine in ourselves is central to our ability to love ourselves. While the move to love oneself is crucial for all Black Christians, it is particularly liberative for Black women, who have had to endure race, gender, class, and at times sexual identity oppression. Black women are uniquely marginalized in the United States, and viewing themselves as created in the image of God and as beings worthy of a deep and permanent love-of-God and love-of-self is an essential step in their healing process. To be sure, some African American Christian women may find that it "sounds odd" to refer to God as "She," because coloniality has undermined their ability to see themselves as genuinely created in God's image. However, as Baker-Fletcher asks, "If God does not identify with Black women, what kind of God is that?"[38] If we believe that God is love and that Jesus is God incarnate (God as dust), then we must also recognize the holistic nature of God in Jesus, who identifies with all humanity through his enfleshment.

SOLIDARITY

As previously stated, the norm that makes this theological anthropology decolonial is the nonnegotiable theological principle that all creation has sacred worth and no created being should be exploited in the eyes of God. Building upon the claim that we should view Jesus as a perfect example of the praxis of being human, I contend that human beings imagine God only insofar as we model ourselves after the perfected image of Christ Jesus. When we model our lives after the life and teachings of Jesus, we are working toward actualizing the potential of being created in the image of God as it has been revealed to us in his life and teachings. A decolonial theological anthropology aims to foster relationships with other created beings and the land that mirror the life and teachings of Jesus, whose earthly ministry was to be in solidarity with the marginalized and care for the "least of these."

In her volume on theological anthropology *Enfleshing Freedom*, womanist Catholic theologian M. Shawn Copeland argues that it is critical for all Christians to explore what she calls Jesus's enfleshment because it creates an awareness that Jesus was the subject of empire and reinforces why solidarity was essential to his ministry. Jesus was a practicing Jew who was once a refugee and, as an adult, lived in a territory controlled by Roman political, military, and economic forces. He grew up in Nazareth, a village residing a few miles away from Sepphoris, a once-thriving city that experienced economic woes as the Roman Empire expanded and created a new city, Tiberias, that eroded Nazareth's commercial opportunities. Indeed, under the taxation policies of Herod Antipas, ordinary peasant-fishermen could no longer cast their nets freely from shore and likely had to sell what they caught to Antipas's factories.[39]

Indeed, Jesus lived and carried out a prophetic liberatory message in the tension between resistance to empire and the desire for the reign of God. The spiritual path of Jesus developed as a way to resist the colonizing forces of the Roman Empire, and now the decolonial message of the Gospel must be restored. In this way, living in ways that mirror the life and teachings of Jesus means reclaiming his radical message of solidarity by standing with those who are exploited as the "least of these" and pursuing political, social, and economic justice for their sake. Moreover, solidarity as demonstrated in the life of Jesus also pushes us to challenge and denounce oppressive and exploitative relationships while also offering compassion for those who long to repair relationships that they have damaged.

At its core, Jesus's earthly ministry of solidarity as described in Luke 4:18–19 (to bring good news to the poor, proclaim release to those held captive, give sight to the blind, and let the oppressed go free) was the work of liberating marginalized and exploited "others" from oppression. To the Roman Empire, Jesus was just a commoner who lived among the common people, the subjects of the empire whose bodies suffered the pain and angst of empire building.[40] The others, the common people, were at the center of Jesus's ministry: the orphans, widows, the disabled, those who were socially and economically marginalized, the dispossessed were the recipients of his compassionate care and often the focus of his teachings. Jesus made his concern for the elimination of exploitative and oppressive relationships clear in his first major public address, where he stated that we are to "do to others as you would have them do to you" (Luke 6:31). The power of this statement is found in its subtlety. If human actions toward those who have been described as Others mirrored our expectation that those who have been branded as an Other *do not* treat us as an Other, then the theological or anthropological category of "Other" no longer exists. Instead, Jesus called us to recognize that all created beings have sacred worth and are deemed good or very good by God; we all exist in an interdependent relationship.

By othering other created beings (i.e., allowing oppressive hierarchical relationships to persist), we violate the norm of a decolonial theological anthropology that no being should be oppressed in the eyes of God because all created beings have sacred worth. As it relates to addressing the systemic racism in our food system, I suggest that striving to mirror the life and teachings of Jesus should push Christians to be in solidarity with the exploited Others within our food system. This requires that we work toward ending the oppressive human-human and human-nonhuman animal relationships upon which our current food system thrives.

Jesus fostered interdependent relationships by practicing solidarity and including people in his inner circle who would otherwise be outcast. As they relate to oppressive human-human relationships fostered by the food system, Jesus's actions of feeding the multitude (Matthew 14:13–21) reveal how important it is for Christians (and, by proxy, the Church) to work to ensure that all people have access to or are provided with food in order to sustain themselves and their families. Moreover, when we consider the parable of the Great Banquet (Luke 14:21–24; Matthew 22:9–10), we see the importance of eliminating oppressive hierarchies. The host replaces the absent guests with literally anyone from the street, and the banquet table represents the diversity of gender, class, race, and religion. For Jesus, this is how unrestricted neighborly love looks and feels; all are welcome, because all have sacred worth. Understood this way, solidarity can be described as a "discernable structure with cognitive, affective, effective, constitutive, and communicative dimensions. Through the praxis of solidarity, we not only apprehend and are moved by the suffering of the other, but we also confront and address its oppressive cause and shoulder the other's suffering."[41] Through a praxis of solidarity, Christians are called to apprehend and feel the suffering of food workers and farmers as if it was our own so that we might address the suffering of food workers and farmers as if it was our own.

Since our food system exploits not only human beings but also non-human animals and our environments, the praxis of solidarity must include attending to them as well. Moreover, in our effort to dismantle structural racism in our food system, it is critical that we remember that the white racial imagination's conception of "the animal"—developed within a culture of Christian white male supremacy—is the conceptual vehicle that morally and ideologically justifies violence against subhuman (e.g., people of color) and nonhuman (animal) Others.

In order to eliminate rather than just replace the structural evil of racism, we must extend Jesus's call to eliminate the theological and anthropological category of the Other to both human and nonhuman animals. In this way, our relationships with the nonhuman animals within our food system should adjust accordingly.

The praxis of solidarity, as demonstrated by Jesus, shows us that harming another being or ending another living being's life when it is unnecessary for our survival allows the reasoning that justifies an oppressive hierarchical relationship between one group over another to persist. In this way, the killing of nonhuman animals for sport and any unnecessary killing of nonhuman animals for food enable the exploitative logic of coloniality to persist.[42] Thus, if we desire to eliminate oppressive hierarchical relationships, mirroring the solidaristic life of Jesus moves us toward the practice of black veganism.

EXCURSUS: SELF-LOVE AND SOLIDARITY FOR WHITE CHRISTIANS

As noted earlier, the decolonial theological anthropology that I am describing centers on the experiences and embodiment of Black people. And while this new anthropology can apply to all people regardless of their racialization, the ways I have described its implementation center people of color as a means to decenter whiteness. However, my aim is to empower all people who desire to break free from the chains of coloniality's definition of the human person. Much could be gained in antiracist social justice work if white people were able to delink their conception of the human person from whiteness. Therefore, it is essential that I explain how a decolonial solidarity and self-love would look for white folks, given that holistic interdependence asks something similar from all people.

For white Christians who are committed to a decolonial understanding of the human person, embracing the implications of solidarity and self-love requires a different focus. With respect to self-love, the solidaristic life praxis of Jesus, who was willing to empty himself and sacrifice his life for those who were oppressed, is an ideal model for how white Christians could practice mirroring the life and teachings of Jesus. Because of the power of the white imagination to center the white experience as normative, white Christians should focus on emptying the colonial assumptions they have normalized as a means to cultivate a sense of who they are outside of the white imagination. Indeed, in order to love themselves, they to need to discover who they are outside of the hierarchy of coloniality.

Solidarity for white Christians first begins with the cultivation of a critical consciousness wherein their personal experiences or the narratives of their particular group (i.e., gender, race, class, etc.) are no longer universalized as Truth, or the only and correct truth. Seeing those who have historically been dehumanized as full human beings means decentering the white experience and honoring the truth of multiple experiences and discerning what action ought to be taken in light of those experiences. To be sure, this is not to say that the white experience doesn't matter or has no significant value for theological reflection. The European American white experience does matter, but the problem is that it has been the only experience that has "mattered" in the construction of what we might call traditional Christian theology. By centering the experiences and narratives of Black, Indigenous, and other people of color, white Christians can gain a deeper understanding of how coloniality shapes our world in ways that are not possible to discern solely through reflecting on how they experience the world.

White Christians must take seriously Copeland's suggestion that "through the praxis of solidarity, we not only apprehend and are moved by the suffering of the other, we confront and address its oppressive cause and shoulder the other's suffering." In this way, for white Christians, solidarity should aim to cultivate an openness that enables them to authentically engage those whom they and their ancestors have historically marginalized. Solidarity then becomes a task, a praxis where responsible relationships between and among persons, between and among groups, and between and among humans and nonhuman animals and nature may be created and expressed, mended and renewed.[43]

Second, solidarity requires anamnesis, the intentional remembering of the exploited, marginalized, and minoritized victims and their historical and ancestral legacy of oppression. Anamnesis requires a retelling of the cultural narratives of Christopher Columbus discovering America, the first Thanksgiving and the relationships between English settler colonialists and Indigenous peoples, the history of African Americans before and beyond enslavement, and the internment of Japanese Americans during World War II, just to name a few. These narratives have been recast through the lens of the hegemonic white racial imagination and suffer from what Dwight Hopkins calls historical amnesia, the intentional misremembering of the past.[44] It has always been more convenient for white Americans and white American Christians to forget (or never ask themselves) questions such as, What happened to those Indigenous peoples who held claim to the land we currently call our own? How was slavery theologically justified as a Christian institution? Why did the end of slavery bring about the Black codes and convict leasing? When did white women acquire the right to vote, and why couldn't people of color vote? Why did the federal government begin to give entitlement (i.e., welfare) payments to corporations? Historical amnesia numbs the conscience and prevents all Americans, especially white Americans, from developing a realistic understanding of the privileges they and their ancestors have been afforded.

Conversely, the solidaristic practice of anamnesis requires a truthful engagement with history. A historical analysis that does not romanticize the past but is intentional about recovering the stories of those who have been oppressed and marginalized is requisite. Moreover, the stories of those whose voices have been silenced are centered, because after being moved by the suffering of another, white people can begin to feel the full weight of the wrongs of their ancestors. While they are not at fault for the mistakes, misdeeds, and evil actions of their ancestors, they now bear the responsibility of reconciliation so that they may begin to heal from the wounds of the past as well.

To be clear, I am suggesting that the stories of the colonial encounters with Indigenous people and Africans should not center on the white experience of the encounter without discerning how that narrative has been used to prop up the myths of white dominance and white saviorism. Indeed, *whiteness has become an idol that all too many Christians worship*, often through the physical or mental image of a white Jesus who looks, thinks, and acts in ways consistent with how evangelical white Christians just happen to look, think, and act. Once the stories of marginalized and oppressed people are accepted as true and meaningful, white Christians can begin to see beyond the lens of colonial Christianity, because the experiences of the oppressed can become the counterframe that enables them to see the world anew.

HOLISTIC INTERDEPENDENCE

Baker-Fletcher's description of Jesus as the embodiment of the perfected image of God adds a crucial liberatory frame to the Genesis Creation narratives. Whereas a basic reading of the narratives suggests that Christians should care for the earth because it is their divinely appointed vocation, Baker-Fletcher's focus on the person of Jesus pushes this claim even further in light of the liberatory nature of Jesus's ministry. She argues that if Jesus was "dust and spirit, like us, then the rest of us humans are likewise called to a holistic relationship with the planet."[45] In this way, accepting that we were created in the image of God and that we are called to imitate the solidaristic love praxis of Jesus allows the spirit of liberation to work within, persuade, and inspire Christians in how we carry out the mission of God to care for the earth, God's creation.

To be sure, caring for the earth and prioritizing a holistic ecological interdependence should not be understood as an attempt to create an egalitarian relationship between all created beings as equals. Thus far, my theological anthropology suggests that Christians' capacity to care for the earth in ways consistent with decolonial thinking can only be accomplished if we live up to the responsibilities of self-love and solidarity that have been conferred upon us. This interpretation of these theological topoi stress the role of human action in dynamic relationship with God, in other words, whom we as God's representatives are called to become and what we are called to do on earth.[46] God continues to realize the aptitude for divinity in all of creation, and despite our imperfections, human beings are unlikely partners. In this way, the relationship between human beings and the rest of nonhuman nature is not equal, nor does it need to be equal.

Following Black Canadian ethicist Peter Paris, I suggest that a distinctive aspect of African and African diasporic ethics is their grounding in a spirituality that unites the spiritual and the natural, thus making all life sacred.[47] This spirituality stands in contrast to Western theological and philosophical thought, which views the sacred as separate from the natural world. Instead, the sacred permeates both human and nonhuman nature. Consequently, the function of human life is a sacred vocation, namely, to preserve and promote the life of the community. Holistic interdependence asks human beings to expand our sense of community to include the more-than-human world. It requires cultivating an awareness that as an interdependent species, our well-being and, indeed, our very lives are dependent upon the health of our ecosystems.

Given the ramifications of structural evil and racism, holistic interdependence (indeed, all environmental ethics) has an anthropocentric orientation within Black and other communities of color because our lives are at stake. Whether the issue is access to clean water in Flint, land sovereignty in Standing Rock, or food injustice in Black communities, it is clear that *environmental practices are always racialized, and racializing practices are always environmental.*[48] To be sure, an anthropocentric focus does not necessarily lead to an oppressive ecological hierarchy. Instead, it requires that we decolonize and redefine the human, the Anthropos, in ways that decenter the colonial logic of whiteness and include women and people of color. I agree with ecofeminist philosopher Karen Warren that there may be "nothing inherently problematic about hierarchical thinking and conceptions and relations of power and privilege *in contexts other than oppression.*" Warren notes that hierarchical thinking is useful in the sciences (e.g., plant taxonomies, biological nomenclature) and that responsible parents may exercise legitimate power and privilege within the household.[49] These hierarchical relationships are only oppressive if a logic of oppression is in place that attempts to justify unjust and exploitative treatment. In this sense, human beings are responsible for caring for the garden of Creation because, among other reasons, we have played a primary role in creating the ecological problems that currently face our planet.

One promising movement that seeks to foster holistic interdependence and break down the artificial barriers between human and natural communities is bioregionalism.[50] Bioregionalism gives us a vision of what earth care could look like for Christians because it encourages people to reinhabit the places they already live in by learning to appreciate the unique attributes of their own communities. Bioregions are defined as distinct geographical areas with specific types of landscapes, soil, native species, and climate. Beyond this, bioregions are also spaces where nonhuman nature, culture, and community intersect. Focusing on such a space gives us a vision of how all life within our communities is deeply connected.

Bioregionalism encourages people to learn about the history of the places in which we live in order to understand how to best live there in ways that do not compromise the fundamental character of the habitat. For instance, planting and overwatering lawn grass in desert climates does not respect the fundamental character of a habitat. Bioregionalism also critiques the urban sprawl that results from the spread of fast-food chains and superstores, "the cultural/economic equivalent of invasive species that destroy native habitats and alter the innate character of landscapes."[51] In this way, bioregionalism attempts to promote a sense of living "in-place," where buying locally grown or produced products and helping to restore native plants and animals to our communities are important goals. Exactly how individuals and churches can accomplish these goals is the subject of the following chapter.

CORN BREAD

Earlier in the chapter, I stated that, given the psychic hold of coloniality, a secondary requirement of decolonization is that we take what Howard Thurman describes as an "inward journey" during which we begin to answer the question, Who are we, really?, to which I add a second question, Whom do we want to be and become? The stories told to us and the ones we tell ourselves shape our answers to these two questions.

The stories of my maternal grandparents and, in particular, my grandfather have played a crucial role in shaping whom I understand myself to be. The story of my paternal ancestry is substantially different but has given shape to the decolonial theological anthropology that I have described. My paternal great-grandfather Joseph Carter was the first Carter to be born in the United States, near Baton Rouge, Louisiana, in 1882. His parents, Antonio and Isadora Caridad, emigrated from the Basque region of Spain in 1881, and sometime after 1919 Joseph changed his last name to Carter.

We don't know a lot about Joe's personality, but we do know that from his midteens until his thirties Joe was an overseer on a sugar plantation along the Mississippi River. An overseer is, more or less, a middleman in the plantation hierarchy, a typical position for a white child of immigrant parents and someone whose primary language was Spanish. Joe would have been responsible for driving (overseers are also referred to as drivers) the field hands to work as fast as possible in order to maximize profits for the plantation owner. It was people like Joe who drove my Grandpa Robert to work so hard that he now deals with crippling back pain. Ultimately, Joe was the white child of Spanish immigrants who likely believed he was doing the best he could, given the vocational choices afforded to him. However, despite his Roman Catholic faith, he was seemingly unable to see Black people as full human beings and worthy of being treated in the same way he was.

We cannot escape our stories, no matter how painful or off-putting they are. Within these ancestral stories we discover the ability to ground ourselves in the sacred source of compassion that sustains us all. In these stories we glimpse the truth of who we are, and it nourishes our soul. We find courage and strength in the stories of our ancestors who made a way out of no way. And for those of us whose ancestry includes folk who enabled the dehumanization of Black, Indigenous, and other people of color, we too glimpse the truth of whom we can become (or continue being) if we do not attend to the broken Christian theological anthropology that informs our social ethics. It is from this grounded awareness of who we are and whom we aim to become that we are able to discern what actions we might take to resist food injustice in our communities. If our actions are to mirror the radical compassionate actions of Jesus, then we must decolonize what it means to be human such that being human is understood as praxis, a process of learning, applying, and realizing our humanness in antioppressive ways.

Joe's story lives within me, and attending to his story is one reason why I have tried to fashion a decolonial theological anthropology that addresses both people of color and white folks. My story is one of the colonized and the colonizer, oppressor and the oppressed. Understanding my story through the lens of compassion helps me understand that all people are entangled in the web of coloniality. The vast majority of people, including white people, suffer at the hands of the psychic grip of whiteness. If our species is going to survive another two or three generations and beyond, all people, but especially white people, must let go of whiteness as a way of being human and begin to understand that being human is praxis. Decentering whiteness in the construction of decolonial theological anthropology does not require white people to abandon their identity. Rather, it asks them and all people to abandon whiteness as a colonial worldview that marginalizes all but a small percentage of life on earth.

Through our revisioning of the human person we can begin to answer Thurman's second question, Whom do we want to be and become? Self-love, solidarity, and holistic interdependence rooted in Black spirituality both inform whom we long to be and whom we long to become. In centering these three theological principles, we lay the framework for an environmental ethic that recognizes that all life has sacred worth and that we human beings have a sacred vocation to care for our communities. Moreover, our notion of the community must include the more-than-human world if we are to attend to the human / animal / nonhuman nature tensions that are the ideological foundation of white supremacist thinking.

For Christians, the interdependence of all life is made explicit in Jesus's last supper with his disciples, during which he shared his body and blood through the sharing of bread and wine. This vegan corn bread serves as a reminder that all creation, human and more-than-human, finds redemption in the body of Christ. If the table of Jesus included those who were othered during his life on earth, wouldn't it follow that Jesus's invitation would extend to nonhuman animals and nonhuman nature because they too are among the dispossessed? "Solidarity sets the dynamics of love against the dynamics of domination." The logic of othering, of domination, is anathema to the Gospel.[52] Indeed, as it relates to food justice for our communities, a decolonial theological anthropology enables us to see that a just food system is possible *and* divinely appointed.

Ingredients
  6 tablespoons water
  2 tablespoons ground flax seeds
  1 cup all-purpose flour
  1 tablespoon vital wheat gluten flour
  1 cup cornmeal
  ¼ cup sugar
  4 teaspoons baking powder
  ¾ teaspoon table salt
  1 cup almond milk
  ¼ cup canola oil

Directions
  Preheat the oven to 425°F. If using a 9-inch cast-iron skillet (like Grandma used) or baking stoneware, place it in the oven while it preheats. Bring the water to a boil in a small saucepan and add the ground flax seed, reduce the heat to medium low, and simmer for 3 minutes or until thickened, stirring occasionally. Set it aside. In a medium bowl, whisk together the flours, cornmeal, sugar, baking powder, and salt until well-combined. Add the ground flax seed mixture, almond milk, and canola oil to the flour mixture. Beat just until smooth (do not overbeat) and set aside to rest for about 10 minutes. Coat the bottom of the baking pan with nonstick spray and pour the mixture into the pan. Bake for 20 to 25 minutes, or until a toothpick inserted in the middle comes out clean. Cool the bread for at least 10 minutes prior to eating.

Chapter 4
Tasting Freedom

> In a Los Angeles project . . . students grow their own
> vegetables to produce fresh, homemade salad dressing
> for local markets, affording them hands-on experience
> of nature, nurture, and economics. That such projects
> exist is a source of hope. I wonder how to make them
> more widespread, beginning in our local communities.
> The next step, it seems, is to consider how such
> projects could be a normative aspect of public
> policy or church agendas. It is important to begin by
> thinking small. If we think big right away, it all seems
> overwhelming and undoable. Once we begin with the
> small projects, however, it seems that we must gradually
> move on to concretely address the larger issues.
> —Karen Baker-Fletcher, *Sisters of Dust, Sisters of Spirit*

In the quote above, womanist theologian Karen Baker-Fletcher describes the experience of many environmental justice activists. For
example, one such activist may have marshaled all of her resources and
successfully started a community garden. Yet, even with this victory, the
activist knows that there is so much more work to be done.

This painful reality often results in the activist's responding in one
of two ways. The first response may be to feel overwhelmed. In regard
to food justice, the community garden is a good start. Not only does
it teach the gardeners a discernible skill, but it also teaches them
patience, care, and the knowledge that, with proper care, their plants
will grow. However, the activist knows that this particular garden can

only bring about so much change and that change will most likely only occur within the community without significantly disrupting our unjust food system. The second response is to feel stuck in the solution-development stage of change-making. Indeed, social justice activists who are stuck in this stage are likely spending their time thinking about how to solve a justice issue; this type of discernment is essential if we are to develop creative solutions to the injustices within our communities. However, I describe these activists as stuck because they are often aware that their proposed solutions are not quite perfect and thus think it best to postpone publicly proposing any solution for fear that it may be disregarded in public, activist, and academic spheres.

I sympathize with these activists because I, too, have felt either overwhelmed by food injustice or paralyzed by the fact that there is no one "perfect" solution. However, in the spirit of John Wesley, the founder of the Methodist tradition within which I am ordained, I understand perfection as a goal Christians should strive toward, knowing that, although we may not reach it in this lifetime, we evolve into more just beings in the process of our journeys.[1] What is more, this is why Baker-Fletcher's emphasis on thinking small and taking small steps is so useful: each step is a journey toward a closer approximation of what we hope will be a perfect more solution. Her thinking exemplifies the idea that being human is praxis, a process of learning, applying, and realizing our humanness in antioppressive ways.

Discerning what actions one might take to practice being human in antioppressive ways is not always a straightforward exercise. The suggestions I outline in this chapter not only are the result of my own discernment but also have been developed in conversation with countless parishioners, friends, family, and colleagues. While one of the practices seemed obvious to me (soulfull eating) for reasons I will describe below, the other two practices have evolved and been refined over the past few years as I continued to discern the best ways religious communities could become institutions that bring culinary and agricultural life to their communities.

The religion of Jesus invites us to be instruments of God's love and compassion through the praxis of being human. We must never forget that Jesus's spiritual path of radical compassion emerged from within a world similar to the contemporary American sociopolitical climate of indignity and corrupt government agencies that enable or encourage structural evil. Jesus lived as a colonial subject of the Roman Empire, whose policies of violence, enslavement, and brutal taxation burdened his community. From within the midst of this oppressive system, Jesus emerged as both a spiritual teacher and a social prophet. He promoted a vision of a beloved community where the social sin of poverty has been eliminated, those blind to injustice are able to see the error of their ways, and those who are oppressed are liberated from their suffering.

Jesus's spiritual path of radical compassion reveals first that our responses to structural evil must be grounded in God's love as the source of truth and power. Second, acts of radical compassion in the face of violence must promote and preserve the flourishing of the humanity of both the victims and the offenders. In this way, our understanding of the human person is informed by the example of the spiritual path of radical compassion Jesus modeled for his disciples. Self-love, solidarity, and holistic interdependence form the basis of a decolonial understanding of the God-human, human-human, and human–nonhuman nature relationships. Remaining grounded in the truth of these three pillars empowers us to imitate Jesus in our fight against dehumanizing racism and mirror Jesus's radical compassion even in the midst of structural evil. To that end, my use of virtue language is intended to serve as the moral and linguistic framing that can help us embody a decolonial way of knowing, thinking, and being in response to food and agricultural injustice.

The purpose of this chapter, then, is to describe and explore three theologically grounded food and agricultural practices that I have developed for addressing the structural racism in our food system. While the practices are described and framed using Christian language, my hope is that any person, regardless of religion or race but moved by the stories of those victimized by our food system and committed to building an antioppressive and antiracist society, could adopt these practices as well. Before concluding the description of each practice I address some potential concerns and criticisms that some may find in my suggestions.

DECOLONIAL PRACTICES AND MORAL VIRTUE

I agree with Christian ethicist Peter Paris in his book *The Spirituality of African Peoples,* where he suggests that practices that form virtuous behavior are practical in every sense and an effective method for pursuing justice.[2] Not only is the language of virtue and social justice in many ways consistent among "African peoples," but the transformative actions of Black food and environmental justice leaders such as Sue Bailey Thurman, Michael Twitty, Fannie Lou Hamer, Heber Brown, Wangari Maathai, and Leah Penniman exemplify that virtuous behavior has been a successful strategy for creating social change.

The importance of virtuous practices is particularly critical in the pursuit of decolonization. Coloniality is a way of knowing, thinking, being, and doing that normalizes the logic, culture, and structure of our Eurocentric modern world system. For most Americans, Europeans, and much of the so-called developed world, the pervasive nature of coloniality has become a habit, a disposition from which we make sense of our everyday encounters and justify the exponential social, educational, and economic inequality within our society.

Decolonization, then, requires the cultivation of virtuous habits (i.e., ways of knowing, thinking, and being) that enable us to discern whether our actions are consistent with our liberatory and antioppressive goals. Consistent with all theories of moral virtue, the virtues discussed below are not innate and are acquired through habitual practices. In turn, these habits eventually produce character traits that dispose people to do certain kinds of virtuous things.[3] To be sure, the power of colonial thinking is that we have been socialized in ways that numb us to the everyday oppression of others: *coloniality often feels normal.* Undoing the habit of colonial thinking requires us to develop new habits, to be open to consistent self-examination, to leave space for self-compassion during the inevitable moments when we notice ourselves falling short, and to offer compassion to others as they move through their decolonial journey.

There are three moral virtues that are particularly important for the decolonial food and environmental justice practices I describe below: practical wisdom, improvisation, and justice. Practical wisdom (or prudence) is excellence of thought and practical reason that guides good action. Paris states that "this virtue pertains to the measure of cognitive discernment necessary for determining what hinders good action and what enables it." As such, practical wisdom allows a virtuous person to discern the middle ground between vicious extremes. Most importantly, the person of practical wisdom is "able to relate the values of the tradition appropriately to particular situations."[4] A practically wise person avoids fundamentalism and pays attention to complexities and particularities of context. Practical wisdom is the exercise of the art of discernment. Practical wisdom enables us to practice soulfull eating, seeking justice for food workers and caring for the earth in ways that are context- and agent-specific.

Although moral virtues are formed by habitual practice, imitation alone does not produce a morally virtuous person. Actions must be done for virtuous reasons. A morally virtuous person is one who exercises good habits, and, conversely, the exercise of good habits constitutes a person of moral virtue. In this way, the practice that cultivates the virtue must become second nature to the individual, and in so doing, they exhibit a novelty that becomes unique to the individual. Paris notes that "although African and African American families have high regard for tradition," social circumstances such as poverty have catalyzed the improvisational skills of Black people. Indeed, Black people have expressed our disposition toward improvisation in the common cultural saying that we often have to "make a way out of no way." The moral virtue of improvisation allows persons to balance both the old and the new, to bring novelty to the familiar, and to creatively solve problems. "By keeping the old and new close at hand, the virtue of improvisation embraces and enhances the whole and thus serves to promote and preserve the goal of community."[5] While necessary for all three practices, improvisation is especially crucial for soulfull eating and seeking justice for food workers.

The final moral virtue, justice, is the supreme virtue because it is the sum of all the virtues, and one "cannot be just without possessing all the other virtues because complete justice would be diminished by the lack of any one of them."[6] Thus, the virtues of practical wisdom, improvisation, and those not treated here are all practical activities, the exercise of which contributes not only to one's own good but also, more importantly, to the good of the community. The ultimate goal of justice is the good of the community. To be sure, communal justice does not need to conflict with justice due to individuals. In being in solidarity with one another and aware of their holistic interdependence, Black communities accept a substantive role in that a community is expected to assume the well-being of its members. With regard to food and environmental justice, the moral virtue of justice provides the ethical orientation (the preservation and promotion of community) that informs the three food and agricultural practices.

PRACTICE: SOULFULL EATING

Soulfull eating asks African American Christians to reflect upon our past and build on the collective culinary wisdom of our ancestors in order to forge a new future of soul food. In this sense, eating is soul*full* because it asks African American Christians to embody Black soul in how we eat. Remember that soul is the vivifying energy (the spirit) of our ancestors, as well as the experiential wisdom gleaned from our foremothers and forefathers that taught Black people how to navigate a foreign land. Soul also means surviving in the midst of oppression without losing sight of the ultimate goal of thriving. It signifies faith in, hope for, and solidarity with all Black people.

In a similar vein, soulfull eating asks African American Christians to challenge oppressive food cultures that impede the collective goal of preservation and promotion of Black communities and, simultaneously, is an opportunity to remember the historical evolution of the Black culinary tradition from a decolonized perspective. Soulfull eating asks us to remember who we are and whose we are. For African American Christians, knowing that we carry an agricultural and culinary history that extends from West Africa to the Americas and that we are created in the image of God and our humanity is not defined by our adoption of Eurocentric norms and is critical in order for us to determine whom we ought to be and the resources available to help us craft new culinary horizons. The practice of soulfull eating therefore encourages African American Christians to critique the ideological stereotypes that have been projected upon Black folks and Black foodways, creating opportunities for us to refashion culinary identities that are grounded in self-love, solidarity, and holistic interdependence.

I have suggested that in its truest sense, soul food is food prepared by Black people using the collective wisdom of our ancestors. In this way, soul food has never been a fixed set of meals or foods; rather, it has evolved over centuries as Black people created new ways to provide food for their families and communities. Given that an open acceptance of the negative status of "the animal" is at minimum a tacit acceptance of the hierarchical racial system of white supremacy and the state of animal agriculture and how it perpetuates the logic of oppression and the subjugation of other nonhuman animals, eating soulfully asks African American Christians to practice an *agent-specific and context-specific* black veganism. As I will describe below, I use "black veganism" as a signifying term that signals a way of eating that decenters whiteness and coloniality. At its best, soulfull eating avoids the consumption of any animal products but recognizes that in our current food system this is not possible for everyone. Soulfull eating is a practice that people should grow into, and, most importantly, food justice activists ought to commit themselves to creating the economic and environmental conditions that enable all people to practice soulfull eating in its ideal form.

When we consider the evolution of Black foodways and Black culinary traditions, I believe that Black folks may be among the most psychologically equipped and culinarily capable of making such a change. At the same time, however, this does not mean that such a change would be easy, and I recognize that these changes would present economic, social, and cultural challenges to some people. Nevertheless, I contend that the collective ancestral wisdom of Africans and African Americans reveals the spirit of a brave and courageous people who have long been committed to an antioppressive liberation and Black self-determination. African American Christian food choices should seek to embody this rich history of spiritual wisdom.

Soulfull eating is informed by a decolonial theological anthropology, and there are three reasons why I argue that it is an effective response to structural racism in our food system. First, an agent-specific and context-specific black veganism makes an explicit connection to the practice of caring for the earth when we consider the ecological impact of industrial animal agriculture. The 2006 report of the Food and Agriculture Organization of the United Nations on the impac livestock on climate change states that animal agriculture "currently amounts to about 18% of the global warming effect—an even larger contribution than the transportation sector worldwide."[7] Soulfull eating helps care for the earth by, among other things, reducing one's carbon footprint and contribution to global climate change. In this way, it is complementary to caring for the earth and concretizes our anthropological claim of holistic interconnectedness.

Second, the decolonial theological anthropological goal of solidarity asks Christians to work toward ending the oppressive human-nonhuman animal relationships upon which our current food system thrives. Indeed, solidarity suggests that African American Christians embody Christ-like compassion toward nonhuman animals by not harming or killing other created beings unless necessary for our own survival. Moreover, solidarity and holistic interconnectedness push African American Christians to fight against the logic that perpetuates the oppression of Black people and justifies the dehumanization of Black bodies, which is consistent with the logic that justifies the theological practice of othering that affects Black, Indigenous, people of color, and nonhuman animals.

The third and most important reason why soulfull eating is an effective response to the structural racism in our food system is that through the practice of black veganism it *decenters whiteness by making explicit the connection between modern race-thinking and the animal.* Recall that the human/animal divide, as it has been constructed by Western white Christianity during the era of coloniality, is the theological and ideological foundation that supports the framework of white dominance. This construction makes it explicitly clear that our modern delineation of human/humanity and animal/animality was constructed along racial lines. This delineation has been a lingering problem within Christianity because the oppression of Black people was justified through theological norms that viewed non-Christian Black bodies as "Other" and through the anthropological belief that Blacks were less rational and therefore less human than whites. As I have shown, as slavery began to take root in American and European economic systems, whites began using a social Darwinian logic of species hierarchy to rationalize the enslavement of Africans by arguing that we were more "animal-like."

Since then, the animalization and othering of Black bodies have been a tool used to dehumanize Black people in the United States and around the world. Given this, the ideological framework that supports racism and white supremacy and the framework that created our current understanding of "the animal" are deeply intertwined and cannot be adequately addressed independently of one another.

When we consider the pervasive nature of the colonial understanding of the human person as a white heterosexual Christian god-like male and the dehumanizing and exploitative logics used to justify the exploitation of Black, Indigenous, people of color, and nonhuman nature, it becomes apparent why these oppressions are so similar: *from the perspective of the oppressor, all victims, regardless of species, are indistinguishable.* Therefore, enabling structural oppression of any kind to exist within an ethical response to our structurally racist food system is a tacit endorsement of the oppressive logic of white supremacy. Indeed, we cannot merely accept the hierarchical logic of structural oppression that justifies nonhuman animal oppression without also adopting the colonial logic and theological othering that justified Indigenous genocide and African enslavement and that continues to rationalize the oppression of Black and other minoritized peoples.

Soulfull eating aims to disrupt an unjust food system and call attention to the systematic oppression of Black people, nonhuman animals, and nonhuman nature. As such, soulfull eating aspires to cultivate the virtue of justice through the expressive disposition of black veganism as a means to preserve and promote Black communities. By practicing soulfull eating, African American Christians can become persuasive leaders among other religious and social justice organizations that are committed to deconstructing systems of oppression. Practicing soulfull eating always raises questions and generates conversations regarding my dietary abstentions. Generally, in social settings that are predominantly Black, I am frequently asked if I am a vegan for health-related reasons. People are often surprised when I explain that my *Christian* theological convictions lured me to practice soulfull eating and that my strict *black* veganism is the best form of practice. This has led to many conversations about what a decolonial and antioppression movement ultimately entails and why the signifier "black" is crucial to how I practice veganism. These conversations during which the intersectional realities of oppression are made explicit can be a means by which Black Christians inspire other religious and secular organizations devoted to liberation to practice soulfull eating.

Having examined why the practice of soulfull eating requires African American Christians to adopt a vegan diet, we can now move toward describing one way in which African American Christians can practice soulfull eating. Cooking soul food is the best way we can learn what it means to eat soulfully.

Sue Bailey Thurman, a journalist and historian by trade and a social pioneer in her own right, understood the importance of reclaiming and sharing Black identity through food. In 1958, as a member of the National Council of Negro Women, she edited a volume titled *The Historical Cookbook of the American Negro*. What is fascinating about this cookbook is that it defied conventional categorization and adopted what she termed, according to culinary historian Anne Bower, "a culinary approach to Negro history." In so doing, the cookbook is an example of how Thurman embodied the virtue of improvisation by either shedding light on or giving new meaning to old recipes. Recipes throughout the book celebrate famous African American people and events throughout the calendar year. For instance, "the book begins in January, celebrating both New Year's Eve and the Emancipation Proclamation" with a recipe for an Emancipation Proclamation breakfast cake.[8] The contents pages list several similar holidays, such as Juneteenth; historical figures such as Harriet Tubman, Charles Richard Drew, Howard Thurman, and James Weldon Johnson; and recipes that are designed to inspire conversation about the vital work of these people.

Soulfull eating asks African American Christians to continue the work of activists like Sue Bailey Thurman by using food as a means to share their ancestral stories and collective wisdom. Indeed, Black foodways have a vibrant and compelling story that needs to be shared. As such, our bowls and plates become griots, and the foods that we prepare give shape to the stories that we share.

By choosing to subvert the oppressive ideology that cooking is a chore, African American Christians can reclaim Black cookery as a communal activity. Preparing a meal for someone is akin to telling him or her a story about who you are, where you come from, and where you hope to go in the future. Cooking enables us to share our story with our children and becomes a means of passing down the culinary creativity that is African American cuisine. In this sense, cooking as a practice can no longer be understood as women's work—and, in fact, "work" is not the right verb to describe kitchen activities. Rather, cooking and eating soulfully become an experience wherein families can reconnect with each other and their histories and where they can glean spiritual wisdom from the stories about ancestors who made a way out of no way.

In his book *The Cooking Gene*, African American chef and culinary and cultural historian Michael Twitty uses the evolution of soul food and Black cookery as a lens to explore his identity and ancestry. Twitty has hosted cooking demonstrations on southern plantations, where he prepares and shares the beautiful foods that enslaved Africans created, all the while dressed in historically accurate attire and using the same kinds of equipment slaves would have used. This approach is one way that Twitty attempts to embody, honor, and learn from the wisdom of our African ancestors. Memory is the key ingredient in all of his recipes. He writes that his "entire cooking life has been about memory. It's my most indispensable ingredient, so wherever I find it, I hoard it. I tell stories about people using food, I swap memories with people and create out of that conversation mnemonic feasts with this fallible, subjective mental evidence."[9] Cooking enables us to remember and re-member our ancestors and the culinary legacies they have left us. The connective power of cooking soulfully lies in the stories that we share and the songs that we sing while we are deepening our culinary identities.

Despite my arguments, I anticipate several objections and concerns over the practice of soulfull eating, specifically as it relates to black veganism. A few of those objections do merit some attention. One concern relates to the Christian practice of hospitality. Some might argue that not eating animal flesh would require Christians to be inhospitable in cultures where meat-eating may not be tied to an oppressive industrial system like the one in the United States and is therefore *less* oppressive. Religion and environmental studies scholar Laura Hobgood-Oster argues that the roots of radical hospitality in the Christian tradition emerge from the culture of the ancient Mediterranean world, Jewish practices of hospitality, and the importance placed on table fellowship in the New Testament.[10] Passages such as Luke 14, wherein Jesus argues that, regardless of social status, everyone is welcome at the table, exemplify radical hospitality. However, what are we Christians to do if we are guests of someone who offers us animal flesh?

What makes Christian hospitality so radical is that it disrupts perceived power dynamics between parties; the poor, the marginalized, and the othered are welcome at the table to sit alongside those who inhabit places of privilege in society. However, I want to suggest that the concept of hospitality be extended to include the nonhuman animals whose marginalization and exploitation have been justified through the same oppressive logic of coloniality. As Christians, we are called to be hospitable to the least of these, and in our current food system, the majority of nonhuman animals are treated as the least—as merely protein units.

Indeed, when I visit guests and I am offered animal flesh or an animal product that I am aware of, I politely turn it down. To be fair, I have had to do this my entire life, as I am severely allergic to seafood and have had to turn down dishes that included any type of shellfish. Based upon my own experience before and after becoming a vegan, turning down food for health or moral and ethical reasons has not resulted in one party being offended. On several occasions, this has resulted in a conversation about my eating habits, but more often, the host simply offers me something else.

Ultimately, Christianity places the burden of hospitality on the host and not the guest.[11] If one is traveling in a country where eating animal flesh is generally rare and, for the sake of one's presence, animal flesh is being served, it is up to the individual guest to discern if refusing to eat the dish would be considered inhospitable. In this way, there is much at stake that the guest must consider. One would have to weigh concerns of hospitality against concerns about the oppression and marginalization of the nonhuman animal and the food worker. If you are traveling in remote regions where access to healthy food has been limited and you are questioning your own nourishment, this must also be considered. Ultimately, these situations must be resolved on a case-by-case basis, because the circumstances within each case can vary greatly.

I have also argued that a decolonial theological anthropology asks Christians to practice the solidaristic love praxis of Jesus, especially as it is described by Jesus in his sermon in Luke 4. Given this, one might object to veganism because some of Jesus's actions appear to show violence toward nonhuman animals, and Jesus himself most likely consumed fish. Critics of Christians who practice veganism and vegetarianism often point to Mark 5, where Jesus met a man possessed by "unclean" spirits, and, upon recognizing Jesus, the spirits asked to be sent into a herd of swine rather than being destroyed. The spirits then entered the two thousand swine, which subsequently stampede off a cliff and into the sea. One interpretation of this passage is that Jesus cares for the possessed man more than the swine and thus allows the spirits to possess the herd even though he knows the swine will die.

However, animal activists Annika Spalde and Pelle Strindlund offer a more fitting interpretation of this passage. According to them, the historical context in which Mark was written suggests that this story could be read as a "coded political tale that grew out of anti-Roman sentiment." Such a reading indeed highlights the anti-Roman imagery woven throughout the passage. For instance, the spirits called themselves *legion*, a term used for the largest Roman military unit. The pigs beg Jesus not to "send them out into the country," and given that pigs are unclean animals in the Jewish tradition, the pigs could be viewed as "unclean conquerors" that had colonized Jewish territory. The fact that Jesus defeated "legion" makes it all the more plausible that readers should interpret this passage as a sociopolitical message designed to inspire its hearers by communicating that they could defeat the Roman occupiers rather than a passage indicating Jesus's lack of concern for swine.[12]

If we move beyond the story in Mark 5, we see that there are many passages within the Gospels that describe Jesus as profoundly caring for nonhuman animals. In Jesus's Sermon on the Mount, he speaks of God's abundant provision for the "birds of the air" and the "lilies of the field" (Matthew 6:25–30). Later he states that although two birds may be sold for a penny, "not one of them falls apart from your Father" (10:30).

Yet despite his care, we do know that Jesus ate fish, and many Christians assume that he also ate lamb at the Passover meal with his disciples. The most important meal in the Christian tradition is Jesus's last supper with his disciples, a meal where lamb would have been traditionally served. However, philosopher and theologian Stephen Webb points out that neither the Gospels nor any secondary sources reference the consumption of lamb at the Last Supper. Webb argues that the simplest hypothesis is most likely the truth: lamb was not mentioned because it was not served.[13]

Regarding Jesus eating fish, systematic theologian Andy Alexis-Baker argues that the position of "Jesus ate fish, I can too" is a fallacy unless we plan to argue that fish is the only nonhuman animal we have grounds to eat. When we consider that the industrial-scale fishing industry and factory fish farms have devastated aquatic life due to disease and genetic engineering, eating a "pescatarian" diet would still support the logic of oppression. Additionally, as Alexis-Baker reminds us, we are called to exercise discernment and therefore embody the virtue of practical wisdom as we live out our goal of solidarity. While a liberative Christianity asks Christians to love, serve, give of ourselves, and resist oppression just as Jesus did, it does not ask us to literally imitate Jesus in terms of itinerancy, dress, modes of transportation, or diet.[14]

When we think about Jesus eating fish, it is essential to remember the vast differences in food access between most Americans and a poor Jewish teacher in first-century Palestine. Jesus lived during a time when access to food, particularly protein, would have been limited based on his economic status. Given that Jesus is fully human and fully God, it is reasonable to assume that he needed to eat a certain amount of protein for a healthy diet, just as we do. However, most people in the United States have abundant access to protein. A 2010 National Health and Nutrition Examination Survey found that on average men consume almost twice and women consume approximately two-thirds more protein than necessary on a daily basis.[15]

To be sure, there are some people (like my grandpa Martin in his youth and my mother during my childhood) who lacked access to an adequate supply of food to feed their families. Being a semisingle parent with three children, my mother both received and purchased food stamps from others in order to ensure that our family had something to eat. During our visits to the food bank, we often received canned meats and sometimes frozen chicken or ham. I find a distinct similarity between Jesus and my mother in this situation. Both of them did what they needed to do to survive; Jesus most likely needed a certain amount of protein, and my family needed whatever food we could get.

In light of the nutritional circumstances faced by some people, eating meat in situations where one's choices are limited could indeed be understood as soulfull eating. Given the death-dealing impact of structural racism within our food system, *soulfull eating must be agent-specific and context-specific.* In other words, your financial and physical well-being are relevant factors in determining how you can practice soulfull eating. For some, veganism will be challenging because they do not have access to the foods necessary to eat a vegan diet. For others, their struggle with diet-related illnesses such as diabetes and heart disease may give them pause. While a vegan diet has been shown to greatly benefit the above-mentioned conditions by the *American Journal of Clinical Nutrition*, in these circumstances, the adoption of a vegan diet must be made in concert with medical professionals.[16] In these cases, vegetarianism may well be the best option for some as we work toward fashioning a more just society where everyone would have access to fresh and healthy food.[17]

In the case of my mother, her actions reveal her disposition toward the moral virtue of practical wisdom. She leaned on the wisdom of her ancestors and stretched every dollar and every meal as far as she could. In doing so, she showed love for herself and her family. She also exercised stewardship over her resources and was careful not to waste anything. Ultimately, my mother was a victim who learned and implemented important survival tactics within an oppressive food pyramid scheme. Unfortunately, there are countless others who still face the same struggle, and it is difficult to predict how many among them are African American Christians. Given that 24 percent of Black adults live in poverty, compared to 20 percent of Hispanics and 10 percent of whites, it is more likely that African American Christians may struggle more than others with a vegan diet due to these economic constraints more so than dietary preference.[18] As such, it will be vital that church communities practice caring for the earth in ways that will be described below, ways that encourage churches to grow food for their communities to help feed others.

The aims of soulfull eating are the preservation and promotion of community and solidarity and the decentering of whiteness in our diets.

While black veganism is an ideal path toward the realization of those aims, soulfull eating must not fall into a rigidity that could potentially produce a moral hierarchy among Black people. As human beings in the West, we are all mired in an unjust food system, and in some ways, we are all complicit in the oppression of others; moral purity is not an option, nor should it be a realistic goal. Rather, our goal must be to dismantle the logics of coloniality, reduce ecological harm, and promote sustainable ways of being in the world. In this way, how individuals and institutions choose to practice seeking justice for food workers and caring for the earth will play a critical role in increasing food access to those who would struggle with the economic and access implications of soulfull eating.

PRACTICE: SEEKING JUSTICE FOR FOOD WORKERS

My second theologically grounded practice is seeking justice for food workers. Throughout this book I have sought to provide a clear view of the oppressive nature of the food system and how the interlocking logic of our colonial food system marginalizes people of color, the global poor, nonhuman animals, and nonhuman nature and especially those who work within the food industry. Indeed, seeking justice for food workers is one way African American Christians can address the racialized economic exploitation that fuels coloniality. Promoting justice for food workers seeks to humanize food workers in both factory and large industrial farms who are generally people of color and/or immigrants whose stories of exploitation are largely unknown.

Domestically, industrial agriculture has had a devastating impact on the economic viability of rural America. Large corporations have purchased many family farms, which has resulted in their near extinction. In 1950 40 percent of rural America lived on farms, while today the number is less than 10 percent.[19] Consequently, as small family farms continue to be purchased by large agribusiness conglomerates, the local goods and service providers that used to populate these small rural towns have disappeared along with them, which paved the way for low-wage nonunionized warehouse superstores to fill in the gaps of food access and employment.[20]

The loss of comparable economic opportunity to that of farming has also resulted in counties containing "factory farms reporting higher rates of food stamp usage than similar counties" that do not have such farms.[21] Proponents of industrial agriculture often argue that factory farms bring jobs to these areas, and they are correct. However, these proponents conveniently fail to mention that these new jobs are low-paying and involve at times dangerous work that rarely lives up to the promises made by those who chose to place the factory in that particular community. Within the United States, many of the people who accept these jobs are immigrant workers who have various reasons for avoiding confrontation with their employers. Additionally, international WTO policies that promote industrial agriculture and free trade are just as disempowering; recall that such policies have forced many small farmers to take their lives or to abandon the land for the city, only to be greeted with unemployment or very low income jobs. The new employment opportunities are nothing more than various iterations of environmental job blackmail, designed to allay the initial storm of criticism corporations and local governments are likely to face from farmers.

The practice of seeking justice for food workers must address this "hidden" cost within the food system. Indeed, in striving to imitate the life and teachings of Jesus by being in solidarity with marginalized peoples, the solidaristic love praxis demonstrated by Jesus toward the exploited workers of his time reinforces the importance of seeking economic justice for food workers. This importance is reinforced when we remember and share the stories of our ancestors whose exploitation helped build the infrastructure of our current food system. To be sure, my maternal grandfather's experience as a migrant farmer whose earliest memories are of plowing fields for twenty-five cents per hour when he was a child has inspired me to work toward changing our food system.

For African American Christians, seeking justice for food workers in day-to-day life encourages activities such as purchasing fair trade grocery items, committing to purchase produce from a community-supported agriculture (CSA) agency, and supporting local grocery store cooperatives. Some CSAs are focused on providing fresh produce at low costs to marginalized communities. For example, Community Services Unlimited, an organization based in South Los Angeles, not only has found creative ways to keep its produce prices low but also offers a delivery service to those for whom transportation is an issue.[22] Perhaps the most impactful way for churches and connectional denominations (e.g., Catholic, Presbyterian, United Methodist, African Methodist Episcopal, etc.) to practice seeking justice for food workers is to create alternative opportunities for employment outside of the oppressive food economy. In the following pages, I highlight how one of the leaders of the civil rights movement, Fannie Lou Hamer, models an example that congregations and denominations could follow.

From a political perspective, justice for food workers encourages African American Christians to become active agents in the political food landscape. Food activism should begin within their respective communities and then their churches and subsequently move outward as they refine their political skills. Activities such as petitioning for the creation of a farmers market in the local community, ensuring that the farmers market accepts state food benefits (i.e., food stamps), and advocating for increased SNAP benefits and minimum wage are essential steps in the fight for food justice. Additionally, churches will need to work with nonprofit agencies such as the Food Empowerment Project to gather information about the types of foods that are "cruelty-free" and then petition their local stores to begin carrying the items.[23] But as Karen Baker-Fletcher reminds us, African American Christians should start small to gain momentum, and as their advocacy skills improve, the scope of the project can increase.

On an international level, seeking justice for food workers urges African American Christians to advocate against policies that monopolize international trade or inhibit marginalized communities in other nations from obtaining food sovereignty. For instance, an examination of the United Nations research on women farmers reveals that women are a critical component of the Third World agricultural economy, even though they receive only a fraction of the land, agricultural training, and economic support (i.e., credit) that men receive: "Women, on average, comprise 43% of the agricultural labor force in developing countries and account for an estimated two-thirds of the world's 600 million poor livestock keepers."[24] In Africa, women constitute 52 percent of the total population, yet they make up about 75 percent of the agricultural workforce and produce and market 60–80 percent of the continent's food supply.[25] As a whole, women produce more than half of the world's food and provide more than 80 percent of the food needs in food-insecure households and regions. These data show that from a global perspective, food justice is directly linked to women's economic and civil rights. Given this, we should not be surprised that pioneering civil rights activist Fannie Lou Hamer was deeply engaged in the food justice movement during her lifetime.

Fannie Lou Hamer's Freedom Farm Cooperative (FFC) is among the best examples of Black self-determination through agriculture. Having grown up poor, food insecure, and politically disenfranchised, Hamer argued that Black agriculture could become a means of resistance. Hamer founded the Freedom Farm Cooperative in 1967 as an antipoverty organization aimed at creating a self-determined, politically engaged, liberated community.[26] Freedom Farm was based in Sunflower County, Mississippi, and it emerged as a social and economic necessity to counter white resistance to civil rights. While Hamer and other civil rights activists were aggressively pursuing the implementation of the Voting Rights Act, the southern white aristocracy was aggressively designing ways to harm any Black person who registered to vote. While the Black residents of Sunflower County experienced threats or actual physical violence for registering to vote, a key strategy for the white male political leadership was to starve the Black residents into compliance with the whites' racial hierarchy. For example, because of the federal agricultural subsidies noted earlier, white farm owners were able to earn money by leaving their land fallow—*the federal government paid them not to grow food!* Consequently, the Black tenant farmers in the county found themselves homeless and without a job.

It was within this social and political space that Hamer developed the idea for Freedom Farm. Hamer designed FFC to concentrate its efforts on three primary areas: "1) to develop an agricultural cooperative that would meet the food and nutritional needs of the county's most vulnerable populations; 2) to create affordable, clean, and safe housing development; and 3) to build an entrepreneurial clearinghouse—a small business incubator that would provide resources for new business owners and a re-training for those with limited educational skills but with manual labor experience."[27] Through fund-raising efforts and the farm's success in its first few years, Hamer was able to purchase nearly seven hundred acres of land. The land was owned and worked cooperatively by about fifteen hundred families. Moreover, while Hamer was firm that the leadership of FFC should be Black, members could be of any race, and more than a few poor white families benefited from this policy. In short, FFC demonstrated how a relatively small leadership team could provide a secure source of food for its members and economic opportunities for those who chose to work the land or manage the sale of their goods.

With the establishment of FFC (among her many other amazing accomplishments), Hamer demonstrated that she intuitively understood that being human was praxis, a process of learning, applying, and realizing our humanness in antioppressive ways. She modeled self-love, solidarity, and holistic interconnectedness in her words and deeds, demonstrating her commitment to the three moral virtues highlighted in this chapter. Her practical wisdom is evidenced in her ability to connect the food injustice inflicted upon her community with the pursuit of voting rights. In so doing, she identified what Rob Nixon terms the "slow violence" happening to the Black residents of Mississippi. Slow violence is "violence that occurs gradually and out of sight, a violence of delayed destruction . . ., an attritional violence that is not usually viewed as violence at all."[28] In describing the condition of the Black residents in Mississippi, Hamer quipped, "Where a couple of years ago white people were shooting at Negroes trying to register, now they say, 'go ahead and register—then you'll starve.'"[29]

Hamer demonstrated her improvisational abilities with the creation of FFC as a response to the slow violence of her community. Like most instances of improvisation, she created FFC in response to the poverty and political disenfranchisement of her community. She sought to bring new meaning to the old industry of sharecropping and tenant farming by reclaiming farming and landownership as critical for Black self-determination. Her disposition to justice is evidenced in her commitment to both community and distributive justice. The members of FFC demonstrated their commitment to the good of the community by supporting the co-op, and the community of FFC assumed responsibility for the well-being of its members.

Hamer's FFC was a radically compassionate approach to addressing food insecurity in her community, a community that included more than just Black people. The FFC model also reveals the necessity of

Black and other marginalized communities to focus not only on food security but also on food sovereignty. Food security is often determined by the presence or absence of corporate supermarkets and thus concedes too much power to corporations that do not have a vested interest in the preservation and promotion of their communities. Food sovereignty focuses on equipping communities to practice democratic control over their food system. The conceptual framework of food sovereignty was defined by the international peasant federation Via Campesina as "people's right to healthy and culturally appropriate food produced through ecologically sound and sustainable methods, and their right to define their own food and agriculture systems." Food sovereignty proposes that communities rather than corporations make decisions regarding their food system.[30] In the coming pages, I will describe how Hamer's model could be duplicated by turning church land into farmland and thus help move food-insecure communities toward food security and food sovereignty.

While some churches may be reluctant to go all in and create a farm cooperative, Hamer's model still provides theoretical insights that can be used by churches to help move their communities toward food sovereignty. One such example is the Black Church Food Security Network, which operates out of Baltimore, Maryland, under the leadership of Rev. Dr. Heber Brown.[31] I first met Brown in 2017 at a food justice conference, and over several long conversations I learned about his work and his vision for the network. The seeds of the network were planted in 2011, when, after visiting another member of his church who was hospitalized due to a diet-related illness, Brown decided that he needed to do more than just pray and offer comfort. He was able to convince his congregation to start a church garden, and, most importantly, he credits the garden as being a mechanism that allowed his older members, who were mostly southern transplants, to share their agricultural wisdom with his younger members who had no idea how to grow food.

The garden was productive and served its purpose of providing produce for his congregation and, on a limited level, the surrounding community. However, the 2015 murder of Freddie Gray by the Baltimore Police Department and the subsequent Baltimore uprising that followed accelerated an idea that Brown had been thinking about for years. The uprising caused schools and convenience stores to close and left his community in an immediate state of food insecurity. Brown connected with Black farmers in Maryland, Virginia, and North Carolina whom he had already been in touch with and asked if he could purchase food from them to resell to his community.

In the years since we first met, the network has grown to include several churches in the greater Baltimore area. These churches host Soil to Sanctuary markets, where Black farmers and urban growers are able to connect with historically African American congregations to create pipelines for fresh produce. More recently, the network has started Operation Higher Ground, which "assist[s] historically African American churches with establishing or expanding gardens or agriculture-related initiatives on church-owned land as a way to improve health, spur economic enterprises, support the environment, and further food equity in local communities."[32]

The Black Church Food Security Network and its leadership demonstrated practical wisdom in the creation of the garden to meet the immediate needs of the community, improvisation to facilitate the development of community markets, and justice by creating an alternative model for Black self-determination outside of the corporate food system. Ultimately, food sovereignty is the best solution to address the structural racism within our food system and the structural evil within the global food system. The Black Church Food Security Network shows us that moving toward food sovereignty is possible in ways that promote the flourishing of Black communities, Black and other people of color, urban gardeners, and Black farmers.

While it is clear that food justice should include seeking justice for food workers, one could question whether African American Christians have enough political power to create substantive change. It is one thing to raise concerns and petition local agencies for changes to local food policy; it is quite another to take on corporate farming and the WTO.

On the local level, African American Christians working in communities of like-minded individuals do have the ability to influence local politicians and municipalities to create policies that benefit food workers in their communities. An excellent example of community members working for food justice in Southern California is the Los

Angeles Food Security and Hunger Partnership (LAFSHP). Though the LAFSHP initially lasted only three years, it reemerged as the Los Angeles Food Policy Council (LAFPC) in January 2011. The LAFPC is a collection of diverse stakeholders, including farmers, gardeners, chefs, food worker advocates, and grocers, among others, who work with the city of Los Angeles to create policies that positively affect the local community.[33] By working with organizations such as the LAFPC and Community Services Unlimited, African American Christians would be better able to aid in creating the positive changes that seeking justice for food workers asks of them.

African American Christians should follow the same model I recommend for addressing local issues on the national level and work with organizations that are addressing national issues related to justice for food workers. Founded in 1962 by the well-known farmworker and civil rights advocate Cesar Chavez, United Farm Workers has been successful in influencing state and national politicians to adopt agricultural reform policies.[34] Additionally, organizations such as the Coalition of Immokalee Workers have successfully lobbied to change agricultural and immigration policies in the United States. Indeed, the practice of seeking justice for food workers would require African American Christians to become active participants in these and similar movements.

An additional concern that one could raise is the tension between caring for food workers and soulfull eating. As I have stated throughout, the oppressive nature of the food system is not only felt by limited access to food; it also affects those who are forced to work in industrial agriculture. Soulfull eating asks African American Christians to practice a context-specific and agent-specific form of black veganism. The tension between soulfull eating and seeking justice for food workers is thus, Should African American Christians continue working on these farms and in these facilities? There are two points that I would like to make in answering this question.

First, justice for food workers who work in factory farms would be finding alternative employment. In this sense, seeking justice for food workers should include individuals and churches helping those who work in factory farms discern and discover other ways of making a living. Fannie Lou Hamer's FFC is one promising model: an urban church could partner with a local agency and help create a small farm, co-op garden, or other agricultural industry. For churches in rural settings, creating an alternative agricultural economy may be easier in regard to access to land. However, their challenge may be confronting the inevitable tension between the industrial farm owner and church leadership.

If creating an alternative agricultural economy as a means of resistance is not a viable option, then helping workers find another vocation would be the next preferential choice. However, there may be some who, for various reasons beyond their immediate control, are unable to find alternative employment. In these instances, African American Christians who work in factory farms would do well to follow the example of Roy Hawkins, the African American waiter who worked at the Coon Chicken Inn. Despite being subjected to racist ideology and the trope of Black men and chicken, Hawkins chose to work at the restaurant because he made a good salary and was unlikely to find a comparable one elsewhere. Likewise, African American Christians who work at industrial or factory farms are responsible for caring for themselves, their families, and their communities, and earning a living is inherently tied to one's ability to provide good care.

An additional concern regarding seeking justice for food workers that one could raise is the impact of black veganism on the factory farm industry. Indeed, if every African American Christian were to practice black veganism, this would clearly have a negative financial impact on factory farm workers and could be understood as a form of harm or even marginalization.

Similar to my mother, factory farm workers are often people who are struggling to take care of their families and are therefore willing to endure hazardous levels of ammonia exposure or the burdensome task of shoving chickens into cages. As Charles Camosy notes, many factory farm workers are immigrants or temporary foreign workers with few resources: they do not speak English, are not unionized, and are therefore less likely to complain or quit even when they are asked to do something illegal.[35]

In the unlikely scenario that factory farming was to collapse, this would undoubtedly hurt many food workers. However, recent human history shows us that economies are capable of shifting to address the

evolving needs of the community. For instance, word processing computers have now rendered typewriters nearly useless, and those who
worked within the typewriter industry were forced to seek other employment. No one would reasonably argue that our society would have
benefited by maintaining our dependence upon typewriters rather
than word processing computers. Likewise, the elimination of factory
farms would provide an immediate benefit to society as a whole by
reducing pollution and eliminating the exploitation of nonhuman
animals and natural resources. The elimination would also provide a
long-term benefit to the factory worker, who is no longer exposed to
the cruel practice of killing another created being.

How will these displaced workers earn a living? This is a legitimate
question, but I want to note that it is often raised under the false pre-
tense that factory farm jobs are a benefit to the community. As I have
argued, this claim is not factually accurate; such job opportunities are
in fact more likely to negatively affect rural economies. With that being
said, if the factory farm industry does collapse, the agricultural sector as
a whole will experience a significant shift in the types of work needed
to sustain a high domestic and international food supply. Workers will
still be needed to grow and harvest food, and the former factory farm
workers could take those jobs, among others.

PRACTICE: CARING FOR THE EARTH

The third practice, caring for the earth, asks African American Christians to cultivate (both literally and figuratively) better relationships
with the land. In my analysis of the creation narratives, I made the case
that farming and food provision are divinely appointed tasks. Indeed,
from a decolonial theological anthropology point of view, a central
aspect of being human as praxis is to embody a holistic interdependence in ways that reflect our capacity to image God. To be sure, the
legacy of slavery and migrant agricultural labor has left a scar on the
psyche of many African Americans. This scar has served to alienate us
from what the biblical writers understood to be the very substance of
human existence: the land. Moreover, alienation from the land has
resulted in a hesitancy among some African American Christians to
care for the earth.

As stated above, the one reason why African American Christians who are committed to food justice should practice soulfull eating is the ecological consequences of factory farms. Factory farms contribute approximately 18 percent of the greenhouse gas emissions that are causing global climate change. Livestock operations produce more greenhouse gases than all the automobiles, airplanes, and ships in the entire world.[36] Additionally, the billions of factory farm animals produce tons of excrement—so much so that some of it gets absorbed back into the land that surrounds the factory. Consequently, everything that goes into breeding a factory-farmed animal—antibiotics, hormones, pesticides, and heavy metals—is currently contaminating our water supply.

In regard to water, factory farm animals require a tremendous amount of water to drink, be cooled, and washed—approximately one trillion gallons per year.[37] When we consider that the World Resources Institute reports that more than 1 billion "people currently live in water-scarce regions, and as many as 3.5 billion could experience water scarcity by 2025," caring for the earth asks African American Christians to stop eating meat as one way to preserve and promote historically marginalized communities.

Caring for the earth and the beings therein also asks African American Christians to advocate for an end to industrial animal farming practices and increased production of plant-based meat alternatives. I have spoken with Ethan Brown, founder and CEO of Beyond Meat, about the potential market for plant-based meat in low-income communities.[38] In conversation with Brown, I learned that it is significantly cheaper to produce plant-based meats when compared to the "meat"-producing capacity of factory farm animals. (As I noted in chapter 3, the true cost of animal meat is hidden from the consumer through corporate welfare that subsidize the agricultural industry.) For obvious reasons, Brown would not disclose to me exactly how his labs create plant-based meat; however, he did explain in general terms what plant-based meat is. Brown stated that "plant-based meat is nothing but a biological composition, a scientific exercise that can be recreated because we know what is in it." Amino acids, lipids, and water constitute the three main ingredients, while carbohydrates and minerals are minor additives. These ingredients are abundant within the plant kingdom and relatively inexpensive when compared to the true cost of nonhuman animal meat. In fact, he contends that plant-based meats (specifically, Beyond Meat's products) could benefit low-income communities by providing them a healthier protein at a lower cost.

Most important for African Americans, Brown is currently marketing his products to grocery store chains that serve low-income and rural communities. Beyond Meat is also committed to addressing climate change and global resource constraints and improving animal welfare by aiming to reduce global meat consumption by 25 percent by the year 2025. Brown's vision for his company makes clear that African Americans' practice of caring for the earth could include supporting companies such as Beyond Meat that are committed to similar ideals.

While it is vital to support companies that are working to increase access to healthy foods, we should not forget that there are many people who cannot afford to buy an adequate amount of food. Religious communities have a long history of feeding the food insecure and as a result have long been invested in alleviating the food insecurity of poorer populations. During my visits to Skid Row while I pastored in Compton, I consistently saw religious organizations providing food to the massive numbers of unsheltered people who call downtown Los Angeles home. Likewise, in all of my ministerial positions, from California to Michigan, I have been involved with community food programs that fed the poor and food insecure. While these activities are essential, practicing caring for the earth asks African American Christians to move beyond food security and to view earth care not only as a way to reconnect with the land and reduce pollution but also as an activity that can help communities become food sovereign spaces.

Gardening and farming are a means by which we honor our ancestors by reconnecting to our agricultural heritage. In this way, practicing caring for the earth promotes the relational and affective dimensions of soulfull eating through the growing of food that could be prepared in community. Practicing caring for the earth allows African American Christians to participate in activities that would enable us to reconnect and reestablish positive relationships with the land such as gardening and farming. By growing some of their own food, African American Christians can begin to address some of the unmet need for access to fresh food if they happen to live in a food desert. While it may be easier for rural or suburban individuals and churches to perform this activity if they are given access to unused land, urban churches can also participate. Churches will have to be improvisational, perhaps utilizing gardening techniques such as planter boxes, wall-mounted planters, and rooftop gardens. Additionally, growing food will allow African American Christians to "get our hands dirty" and reconnect with the soil while working with our loved ones on a project designed to increase food security for ourselves and promote food sovereignty for our communities.

There is an emerging faith and farming movement within the United States. In November 2018 I was the lead facilitator of the Duke World Food Policy Center's inaugural Food and Faith Convening.[39] This meeting brought together farmers, food justice activists, academics, and funders to discuss and envision what the future of food and faith could look like. One of the primary points of discussion was the desire to convince church leaders to use their land as a resource for the community—to turn church land into farm land. Several attendees had attended a gathering of religious leaders, clergy and laity alike, who had successfully convinced their churches to begin farming a portion of their land.[40] The concept of turning church land into farm land could have tremendous impact within Black communities if Black churches and religious leaders begin to see church land as a gift that is for and to be shared with their communities.

There are a few seminaries that are at the forefront of integrating an ecological consciousness and land ethic into theological education, and among those, the Methodist Theological School in Ohio (MTSO) stands out for the ways in which it has integrated an explicit liberatory and decolonial component to its work. Elaine Nogueira-Godsey, assistant professor of theology, ecology, and race at MTSO, describes this pedagogical approach as "decological," a truncation of decolonial and ecological.[41] Seminary Hill Farm sits on over ten acres of the campus. The farm operates a CSA, sells produce to local restaurants, and has been integrated into the campus food service. Pedagogically, MTSO offers courses that help students undo the logic of coloniality by exposing the role whiteness and colonial thinking have played in normalizing the exploitation of farm workers and the land. Most importantly, MTSO is in the beginning stages of discerning how it can become a training ground for religious leaders who want to both learn ecotheology and apply that knowledge by gardening or farming in their own community.

To be sure, reconnecting with nature—and perhaps gardening and/or farming—may be emotionally challenging for some African Americans due to the psychological residue of slavery. Environmental historian Dianne Glave has remarked that "feelings of distaste are long-standing for African Americans whose forefathers and foremothers experienced nature entwined with fear and violence."[42] Stories of enslavement and fieldwork were and still are being told among African Americans, particularly those with deep southern roots. While the stories of our enslavement and forced labor are important and powerful, they ought not be the only stories that we share about our relationship with the land. As I have argued elsewhere, slavery and tenant farming are one source of our agricultural history, but we should not view them as the only source.[43] To do so would be to deny the agricultural legacy outlined in chapter 1, a legacy of ingenuity that Black and white people alike have unfortunately interpreted through the lens of the white hegemonic imagination.

Leah Penniman, the cofounder of Soul Fire Farm in upstate New York, had similar psychological struggles when she felt the vocation call to become a farmer. Penniman notes that as her race consciousness evolved, she felt she had to choose between "traditional" Black activist work concerning gun violence, housing discrimination, and education reform and predominantly white activist work in environmental conservation and organic farming.[44] However, at a gathering of the Northeast Organic Farming Association, Penniman and her colleague Karen Washington gathered the small group of Black farmers in attendance, and they decided to create an alternative conference aimed at bringing together Black and Brown farmers and urban gardeners. The Black Farmers and Urban Gardeners (BUGS) conference began in 2010 and has met annually since.

Through the BUGS conference, attendees learned that our modern notion of organic farming emerges from an African-Indigenous system developed over a millennium ago and first revived by Dr. George Washington Carver at Tuskegee University. Carver's system of regenerative agriculture was developed after extensive research during which he "codified the use of crop rotation in combination with the planting of nitrogen-fixing legumes."[45] Attendees also learned that Tuskegee University's Dr. Booker T. Whatley was one of the inventors of the community-supported agriculture model that is still used today through what he termed the Clientele Membership Club.

Buoyed with this knowledge and the support of her husband and her South End community in Albany, New York, Penniman started Soul Fire Farm. Soul Fire Farm is committed to ending racism, injustice, and food apartheid in our food system. While the farm is not a Christian enterprise, it operates with a deep reverence for the land and wisdom of our African and Indigenous ancestors and "work to reclaim their collective right to belong to the earth and to have agency in the food system."[46] Most impressive is that in the few short years the farm has been in operation, it has had a tremendous impact on the Black farming movement. In 2018, through the farm's various programs, which include a CSA, farmer apprenticeship and training, activist and ally training, and youth incarceration diversion, the farm impacted nearly eight thousand unique individuals.

Ideally, Black rural or urban churches that have access to unused land and are committed to fighting for food justice and moving toward food sovereignty should consider following the Soul Fire Farm model. The resources and educational opportunities available through Soul Fire Farm are invaluable if we are to make peace with and reclaim the land that was taken from us after emancipation through the racist farm subsidy system. Soul Fire Farm's model not only helps move communities toward food security and sovereignty but also creates jobs and training opportunities for the community, which complements the above-described practice of caring for food workers.

The work of Soul Fire Farm is an excellent domestic example of how being human as praxis by embodying self-love, solidarity, and holistic interdependence in ways that undo the grasp of coloniality naturally leads to the practice of the virtues of practical wisdom, improvisation, and justice. The work of Kenyan environmental activist and Nobel Peace Prize winner Wangari Maathai is evidence of the ways nonhuman nature can be a source of healing and resistance for Black people around the world as well.[47] Her practice of caring for the earth emerged out of both her experience as a Black woman and her Christian and

African Indigenous spirituality. To be sure, my account of Maathai's work does not do justice to the immense role that she has played in the environmentalist movement. However, given that the ecological impact of food and environmental injustice affects Black and Brown people across the globe, it is critical that African American Christians look to our sisters and brothers in the so-called developing world to glean insight from the work that they are already doing to combat racism, sexism, and environmental injustice.

In 1977, under the auspices of the National Council of Kenyan Women, Maathai founded the Green Belt Movement (GBM). The goal of the GBM was to help rural Kenyan women reclaim their agency by working together to solve the environmental and economic problems that they all were facing. The women and their families were suffering from a lack of water due to the drying up of streams, a less secure food supply because of the lack of water, and rampant deforestation, which made gathering wood for fuel and fencing a significantly more difficult task. The initial step taken by the GBM to solve these problems was to foster solidarity among the women and encourage them to work as a group "to grow seedlings and plant trees to bind the soil, store rainwater, provide food and firewood."[48] The GBM was also able to provide the workers, the majority of whom were women, some monetary compensation for their work. After a few years running the program, Maathai noted that she had come "to recognize that our efforts weren't only about planting trees, but were also about sowing seeds of a different sort—the ones necessary to heal the wounds inflicted on communities that robbed them of their self-confidence and self-knowledge."[49] In this way, despite the program's initial success, she understood that unless the GBM began to address the deeper issues underlying the social and environmental problems of rural Kenyans, the success of the GBM would be short-lived.

Maathai argued that the everyday hardships of the poor—ecological degradation, deforestation, and food insecurity—were (in some ways) the consequence of social issues related to the disempowerment and disenfranchisement of women and a loss of indigenous values that fostered a sense of communal well-being. Consequently, the GBM created seminars (currently called Community Empowerment Education seminars) to encourage individuals to examine why they felt as though

they lacked the agency to change their social, political, and environmental circumstances. Through these consciousness-raising seminars,
participants developed an awareness that the democratic process in
Kenya viewed them as a political tool and only took their concerns as
seriously as they needed to in order to be elected. Moreover, they realized that by placing their confidence in these elected officials rather
than working toward solving their own problems, they were in some
ways complicit in their own marginalization.

Indeed, Maathai argued that too many Kenyans had forgotten the
African values that their parents taught them as children: to work for
the common good and community well-being as a means of preserving individual security and well-being. She began to reshape the GBM
around four core values that were meant to recapture this indigenous
knowledge: love for the environment, gratitude and respect for the
earth's resources, self-empowerment and self-betterment, and the spirit
of service and volunteerism. Maathai's embodiment of the virtues is
unquestionable. Her commitment to justice is evidenced by her stead-
fast focus on the role of sexism and patriarchy in the economic and
ecological marginalization of women. The idea of planting trees as a
means of cultivating solidarity among the dispossessed while also being a viable source of income shows her ability to improvise and create something new out of virtually nothing. Lastly, she demonstrated
practical wisdom by helping her community remember the wisdom of
their ancestors and apply it to their current situation.

There are a few concerns that one could raise regarding the practice
of caring for the earth. For instance, there may be some individuals
who do not know how to garden because they were raised in an urban
area. Alternatively, perhaps a congregation would like to start a community garden or an urban or rural farm, but their agricultural lineage
has passed away, and they are reluctant to begin an unfamiliar project.
There may be older individuals or congregations who are unable to
perform the physical labor of gardening.

African American Christians with whom I have spoken about my
project have consistently raised these concerns. My solutions, which
I believe can be replicated at any location, are as follows. First, many
urban and rural CSAs have gardening and farming programs that are
offered free of charge to communities, and some of them, such as

Community Services Unlimited, even offer to help nonprofit organizations start their own gardens. While Soul Fire Farm does charge for its training, costs are offset by fund-raising efforts and are intentionally kept as low as possible. Second, youth gardening programs have been hugely successful in primary schools. Congregations that are unable to garden due to physical limitations should pursue partnerships with local schools and after-school programs. These partnerships not only allow younger people to reconnect with the land but also create the space for community building and mentoring through intergenerational conversation.

WATERMELON

When I began to realize that food justice was going to be a part of my personal and professional career, I struggled to discern how I could use my talents to address such a huge problem. I felt overwhelmed and that I wasn't qualified to offer any suggestions because, unlike my grandfather, I have never been a farmer. However, I knew I needed to do something. Grounded in the stories of my ancestors and my Christian faith, I came to realize that my insecurities were a result of my fear of failing and of committing myself to a type of social justice work that is often understood to be white. Resting in the truth of who I am and who God has created me to be helped calm the inner stirrings of anxiety and enabled me instead to feel the suffering of those who suffer from an unjust food system, as my family has, and to feel the guilt of those who benefit from such systems, as my family has. My compassion for these people is built upon the recognition that all life is interconnected and longs to be restored to a right relationship with the divine.

In discerning what compassionate action I might take, Frank Rogers identifies six signposts of compassionate action, three of which I have used to develop the food and agricultural practices in this chapter: solidarity, empowerment, and justice.[50] All three practices contain aspects of the three pillars, and I have sought to emphasize empowerment—providing marginalized members of our society with the skills, tools, and personal capacities to sustain their own flourishing—as a means to move toward a psychological food sovereignty with soulfull eating and physical food sovereignty with justice for workers and caring for the land. Compassion must be at the heart of any food and ecological justice program if it is to be sustainable and transform, preserve, and promote Black communities.

In trying to decide what I would serve that could be either a dessert or an appetizer at my vegan soulfull table, I settled on an already vegan staple of the African American diet: watermelon. In writing this chapter, I was brought back to the summers with my grandpa out in his garden and my current work with community gardens in Southern California. After a hard day's work in the heat, watermelon tastes even better than you remember. Whether you like it plain or sprinkled with a little salt, watermelon is quintessential soul food.

There are so many racist stereotypes projected upon Black folks who eat watermelon that some of you may be surprised that I decided to include it in my vegan soulfull dinner. These stereotypes are, in fact, why I chose to include it. The stereotype of a lazy, watermelon-eating Zip Coon was created by the dominant white culture for two reasons. First, it was intended to allay the fears white men had about Black men taking their jobs postemancipation. Many former slaves grew, ate, and sold watermelons, and in so doing, watermelons became a symbol of their freedom. For whites, rejecting watermelons and inhibiting Black self-determination were akin to rejecting the new social order of emancipation. Second, the stereotype was invented to try and convince Black folks that they were in fact lazy, watermelon-eating Negros.

To be sure, this myth continues to impact me, and I have had to calm the interior stirring that wants me to avoid eating anything that could be perceived as being "too Black" in front of white people by reminding myself that these racist tropes were invented to dehumanize my community. Being grounded in a decolonial theological anthropology and knowing who and whose I am helps me reclaim my subjectivity by reminding myself that these foods center Blackness and decenter whiteness. This act may make some white people uncomfortable, but I am not responsible for soothing white people; they have the capacity to do this themselves. By tending the wounds that these assumptions have had on our personal and communal psyche, we create the space for transformational healing. In this way, eating watermelon with these

ideas in mind and particularly in mixed company could be understood
as an antiracist act when it is decoupled from white supremacist logic.

Similarly, the goal of the three theologically grounded food practices
is to delink from coloniality and decenter white supremacist logic as
it pertains to how we eat. In not defining soul food as a group of fixed
or static recipes and dishes, we ought to be mindful that eating soulfully doesn't necessarily require that we change everything about our
diets. Rather, eating soulfully and practicing black veganism asks us to
extend our antioppressive liberatory faith commitment to our plates. As
such, what soulfull eating looks like will be necessarily context-specific
for individuals, families, and communities. Given the heaviness of the
topic, the light and sweet taste of watermelon may be just what we need.

Conclusion

Food Deserts and Desserts

In its narcissistic monologue the colonist bourgeoisie,
by way of its academics, had implanted in the minds
of the colonized that the essential values—meaning
Western values—remain eternal despite all errors
attributable to [humans]. The colonized intellectual
accepted the cogency of these ideas and there in the
back of [their] mind stood a sentinel on duty guarding
the Greco-Roman pedestal.
—Frantz Fanon, *The Wretched of the Earth*

Decolonization . . . does not mean and has not
meant a total rejection of all theory or research or
Western knowledge. Rather, it is about centring our
[Indigenous] concerns and world views and then
coming to know and understand theory and research
from our own perspectives and for our own purposes.
—Linda Tuhiwai Smith, *Decolonizing Methodologies*

The Spirit of Soul Food is the result of my quest to discern what soul food
should look like today given the structural racism and inequities of
our food system. Ultimately, I conclude that coloniality, the social and
psychological vestiges of colonialism, is a disease that through globaliza-
tion has infected practically every sphere of our lives. Within American
agriculture, the pervasiveness of coloniality has always been explicit:

from genocide to slavery to sharecropping and immigrant labor, it is a system built upon the exploitation of mostly Black and Brown bodies. I believe every Christian, especially every Black Christian, ought to be resisting our structurally evil food system, and I wanted to figure out how I could help us toward that end.

Coloniality has successfully convinced many of us either that some human beings don't deserve (e.g., have not earned the right) to live a flourishing life or that it is socially and economically impossible for all human beings to be afforded a universal basic standard of living. Unjust systems become normalized because enough people believe that ultimately everyone gets what they deserve in America. In this way, coloniality necessarily limits our imagination of what social justice and, for our purposes, food justice can look like. I've structured this book to resist this imaginative limitation. The introduction and chapters 1–3 attempt to dismantle key aspects of the logic of coloniality with respect to food injustice: racism, neoliberal political systems, the erasure of African and Black agricultural and culinary knowledge, and a racist and sexist theological anthropology. The three theologically grounded food and agricultural practices that I propose in chapter 4 are my attempt to demonstrate how a decolonial theological anthropology necessarily leads to the decentering of the ideology of white dominance and the decolonization of our diets. While my three practices are informed by radical compassion, they may have felt more radical than compassionate because I am trying to reject the intellectual confines of coloniality that seek to stifle new and imaginative ways of practicing being human in the world.

Coloniality is the epistemological fountain we drink from when we subscribe to principles that normalize the logic of oppression, the logic that supports white heteropatriarchy. Coloniality is designed such that only a few white people, Frantz Fanon's bourgeoisie, are actually accorded all the privileges of whiteness and of being human. In this structure, all other human beings are placed somewhere on the continuum between humans and animals. Accepting the conclusions that coloniality inevitably brings us to and building an activist agenda in light of those conclusions have proven to be notoriously difficult. Historically, when activist momentum builds to the point where colo-

niality is challenged, a faux humanness is offered in the form of civil
rights, women's rights, LGBTQ rights, and so on. This is not to say
that each of the above-mentioned groups does not deserve civil rights;
clearly, they do. I wanted to highlight the tension that exists when
we view the acquisition of *rights alone* as sufficient victories despite
knowing that these "human" rights are built upon a white supremacist
Christian male logic. We must never forget that within the logics of
coloniality the majority of human beings are not seen as human and
their moral obligations to subhumans and nonhuman animals are
necessarily limited in order to preserve a law and order that protects
white elites. Therefore, as Christians who are directed by the Greatest
Commandment to embody love and pursue just relationships with all
of our neighbors, I want to suggest that we are all charged with the task
of decolonizing our minds, as well as our religious, social, and political
institutions.

Decolonization is the twin process of identifying and dismantling
colonialist logic in all its forms. Decolonization requires seeking out
the hidden aspects of the political, economic, and social ideologies
that maintained colonialist thinking even after political independence
or civil rights have been achieved.[1] For academics and activists trained
within the academy, decolonizing our thinking can be a psychologically
taxing experience. Fanon's quote suggests this when he writes that
"the colonized intellectual accepted the cogency of these ideas and
there in the back of [their] mind stood a sentinel on duty guarding
the Greco-Roman pedestal."[2]

The American educational system teaches us that Eurocentric social,
economic, and political norms are ideally designed but, given the sinful nature of humanity or the ignorance of certain groups of people,
poorly executed. The moment we realize that several of these Eurocentric norms are designed with evil intention is both liberatory and
frightening. It is liberating because we have a clearer vision of where
our intellectual and activist energies must be spent. It is frightening
because decolonization requires an inward journey where we seek out
and dismantle the sentinels that have dutifully guarded the colonialist
logic we have embedded in our psyche. Decolonial thinking requires
that we become aware of the white racial imagination in the cultural

production of evil, the white racial frame that is the lens through which some white people view nonwhites, and how the Black counterframe operates within the logic of coloniality. Decolonial thinking pushes us to develop a counterframe beyond the scope of the oppositional structure of the human/animal binary. When food injustice is viewed through the lens of this decolonial counterframe, the logic that supports food injustice and our complicity within it becomes clear.

With respect to food injustice and decolonial thinking, I have followed the suggestion of Indigenous scholar Linda Tuhiwai Smith and attempted to center the concerns and worldviews of Black people specifically and other people of color in general. In centering the concerns and worldviews of Black folks, I crafted answers to three questions: Who are we? Whom ought we to become? How should we live in response to the answers to those questions?

As people of color in America, many of us either live within or grew up around spaces where food injustice was a part of the everydayness of being alive. Being Black or Latinx in the United States means that we are more likely to suffer from food insecurity, environmental racism, and the legion of health problems that result from this reality. The political systems and regulatory agencies that are in place have not offered adequate protections for people of color in the United States. The global agencies that are tasked with protecting the interests of developing countries have enabled continued colonial and capitalist exploitation. Our global food economy has all the trappings of a pyramid scheme wherein those who economically benefit the most have consistently persuaded the US government that they need more subsidies to feed more people, even as rates of food insecurity continue to rise.

However, being Black also means that we are heirs to a proficient agricultural and culinary past, a past that extends to our African ancestors and is still alive today. Many of our ancestors were sold into slavery because of their agricultural or pastoral acumen. Blacks became among the most accomplished chefs in the world by using techniques learned from both sides of the Atlantic. As Black people, we should be proud of our agricultural and culinary history, but all too often deep feelings of shame emerge when we discuss gardening, farming, or cooking.

Coloniality has caused us to associate agriculture and farming with slavery, and we perceive cooking as a chore, but decolonial thinking can help us reclaim our gardens, farms, and kitchens as sacred spaces where spiritual wisdom is passed from one generation to the next. Indeed, this spiritual wisdom was habituated in African and African American people so they would know how to navigate in a foreign land. Soul signifies *faith* in, *hope* for, and *solidarity* with all black people and challenges coloniality by centering black affective and experiential knowledge.

Being a Black American Christian means that we have inherited a theological anthropology that has sought to mute how Black soul is theologically expressed. If we are going to become Black Christians who embrace Black soul and take seriously our moral obligation to love God, neighbor, and self, then the implications of the God-human encounter must be decolonized. Recall that the human/animal divide, as Western white Christianity constructed it during modernity, is the theological and ideological foundation that supports the framework of white dominance. This means that *our modern delineation of human/ humanity and animal/animality was constructed along racial lines.* As such, in order to become human and practice a Christianity rooted in love and justice, we must redefine what it means to be human outside of the oppositional structure of the human/animal binary. We should not want to become human if being human is understood as acquiescing to the system of white Christian male heteropatriarchy. We should not want to become human if being human means we must adopt the values of an individualistic worldview where humans exist separately and apart from nonhuman nature. Fighting for human equality within this framework is to fight for the right to practice behaviors that are consistent with a flawed theological principle that reinforces hierarchical oppression.

As such, decolonizing Western Christianity's assumptions of the human requires us to view "being human" as praxis, a process of learning, applying, and realizing our humanness in antioppressive ways. Thus, being human means that we revel in the fact that we are children of God. It means that we love ourselves because to do otherwise would be sinful; we love ourselves because we deserve to be loved. Being human also means that we strive to imitate Christ in our commitment to be in solidarity with, to love, and to serve the least of these. The solidaristic love praxis of Jesus is the best example of what it looks like to love in truth and action. Lastly, being human means that we recognize and accept a holistic interdependence with all of Creation. In thinking about food and agricultural justice, holistic interdependence asks us to care for the earth by reclaiming a positive and mutual relationality with the land. For Black Christians, holistic interdependence and ecological care must make explicit the connection between the dehumanization of Black and Brown bodies and the exploitation of nonhuman nature to sufficiently resist ecological injustice. If we are to embrace the Christian call to practice being human, then our moral commitment to an antioppressive liberation requires that we change our thinking in regard to food, nonhuman animals, and nonhuman nature.

Trying to imagine how one might live according to these three theological principles is to wrestle with the realities of colonial thinking. Martinique poet and author Aimé Césaire captures this challenge in his *Discourse on Colonialism*:

> For us, the problem is not to make a utopian and sterile attempt to repeat the past, but to go beyond. It is not a dead society that we want to revive. We leave that to those who go in for exoticism. Nor is it the present colonial society that we wish to prolong, the most putrid carrion that ever rotted under the sun. *It is a new society that we must create . . . a society rich with all the productive power of modern times, warm with all the fraternity of olden days.*[3]

In developing the three theologically grounded food practices of soulfull eating, seeking justice for food workers, and caring for the earth, I did not want to retrieve an ideal past or legitimize our current food systems. Rather, I attempted to imagine what soul food should look like today given the pervasive nature of food and environmental injustice in Black, Indigenous, and communities predominantly populated by other people of color.

The moral virtues that emerged from the Black experience, practical wisdom, improvisation, and, most importantly, justice, are embedded within each practice so that our virtuous behavior is consistent with the goal of preserving and promoting our communities. The black veganism of soulfull eating aims to decenter normative whiteness as a means of reclaiming what it means to be human by defining our humanity in ways more consistent with the Christian faith than Western white theological anthropology has proven to be. Seeking justice for food workers seeks to humanize agricultural and factory farm workers and argues that churches should play a critical and even vocational role to ensure this happens. Caring for the earth pushes us to see our interdependence with Creation and embrace our Christian vocation of ecological care.

The problem of food and ecological injustice is pervasive both domestically and globally, and the suggestions I propose are designed to attend to some of those problems. However, my suggestions alone are not enough to upend the global food economy in ways that will force it to become just; my ideas could have an impact, but they are only the germinating seeds of revolutionary thought. My hope is that the framework I have outlined in this book will also inspire activists to imagine solutions beyond the scope of my own suggestions and bloom in ways that lead to a just global food system. For the marginalized, liberation and decolonization from the oppressive food system will be a dynamic process. Our actions and practices will have to evolve even as the white supremacist culture evolves its methods for thwarting our social and political actions. Consequently, a fundamental goal in this process is thinking about how food justice can become a normative aspect of antioppressive liberatory African American Christianities.

The last dish of our soulfull table, peach crisp, signifies my pursuit of a vegan dish that would pay homage to the peach cobbler that was commonly served during the large family gatherings of my childhood. For me, eating dessert always signaled the end of my time with family and friends. In some ways, it encourages the reflexive response to reflect on the time spent with loved ones and to savor the sweetness of their company. As you look back on the arguments laid out in this book, my hope is that, more often than not, you find them both sweet and satisfying. And in so doing, you might be reminded that soul food, served one plate at a time, should be among our most potent weapons to decenter whiteness, resist white supremacy, and preserve and promote Black community and solidarity.

Peach Crisp

Ingredients

Peach Filling
  2 pounds frozen peaches, partially thawed
  2 tablespoons cornstarch
  ½ cup agave nectar
  1 teaspoon vanilla extract

Crumb Topping
  ¾ cup oatmeal
  ½ cup unbleached all-purpose flour
  1 cup brown sugar
  3 tablespoons cinnamon
  ½ cup sliced almonds
  12 tablespoons vegan butter, diced small and placed in the freezer for
  15 minutes

Directions

Preheat the oven to 375°F. In a large mixing bowl, sprinkle the peaches with the cornstarch and toss lightly until they are well coated. Pour the peaches into a large sauté pan, cover, and cook on medium heat. Add the agave nectar and vanilla and stir until the liquid is simmering and thick. Remove the peaches from the heat and set aside. Place all the ingredients for the topping into a 1-gallon plastic sealable bag. Break up the butter with your fingers, then smash and shake the bag until the mixture is crumbly. Place the peaches, including the liquid, in a lightly greased 9-by-9-inch baking dish. Evenly cover the peaches with the crumb topping. You should have some topping left over; freeze it for future use. Bake the peach crisp for about 40 minutes, or until the peaches are bubbling and the topping is firm and brown.

Notes

Preface

1. Seth Schoen is the cocreator of Racial Resilience (www.racialresilience .com), an antiracism seminar that utilizes the combined insights of compassion-based contemplative practice and critical race theories.

2. Frank Rogers Jr., *Compassion in Practice: The Way of Jesus* (Nashville: Upper Room Books, 2016), 21.

Introduction

1. Robert Gottlieb and Anupama Joshi, *Food Justice* (Cambridge, MA: MIT Press, 2010), 6.

2. US Department of Health and Human Services, Centers for Disease Control and Prevention, Office of Minority Health & Health Equity, "CDCP: Minority Health—Black/African American Populations," February 2015, http://www.cdc.gov/minorityhealth/populations/REMP/black.html.

3. Kristin Wartman, "Why Food Belongs in Our Discussions of Race," *Civil Eats*, September 3, 2015, https://civileats.com/2015/09/03/why-food -belongs-in-our-discussions-of-race/.

4. Arline T. Geronimus et al., "'Weathering' and Age Patterns of Allostatic Load Scores among Blacks and Whites in the United States," *American Journal of Public Health* 96, no. 5 (May 2006): 826–33, https://doi.org/10.2105/ AJPH.2004.060749.

5. L. Pan et al., "Differences in Prevalence of Obesity among Black, White, and Hispanic Adults—United States, 2006–2008," MMWR Weekly, CDC, https://www.cdc.gov/mmwr/preview/mmwrhtml/mm5827a2.htm.

6. "Heart Disease and African Americans: The Office of Minority Health," https://minorityhealth.hhs.gov/omh/browse.aspx?lvl=4&lvlid=19.

7. Wartman, "Why Food Belongs."

8. Marjorie Spiegel, *The Dreaded Comparison: Human and Animal Slavery*, revised and expanded ed. (New York: Mirror Books, 1996).

9. Aph Ko and Syl Ko, *Aphro-Ism: Essays on Pop Culture, Feminism, and Black Veganism from Two Sisters* (New York: Lantern Books, 2017).

10. "Herstory of Black Lives Matter," Black Lives Matter, https://black livesmatter.com/about/herstory/.

11. Naha Sehgal, Greg Smith, and Joseph Liu, "A Religious Portrait of African-Americans," *Pew Research Center's Religion & Public Life Project* (blog), January 30, 2009, http://www.pewforum.org/2009/01/30/a-religious-portrait -of-african-americans/.

12. "Religious Landscape Study: The Religious Composition of Blacks," *Pew Research Center's Religion & Public Life Project*, May 11, 2015, http://www.pew forum.org/religious-landscape-study/.

13. Liu, "A Religious Portrait."

14. Walter D. Mignolo and Catherine E. Walsh, *On Decoloniality: Concepts, Analytics, Praxis* (Durham, NC: Duke University Press, 2018), 110.

15. Bill Ashcroft, Gareth Griffiths, and Helen Tiffin, *Post-colonial Studies: The Key Concepts*, 3rd ed. (London: Routledge, 2013), 73.

16. Mignolo and Walsh, *On Decoloniality*, 4.

17. Lewis R. Gordon and Jane Anna Gordon, *Not Only the Master's Tools: African American Studies in Theory and Practice* (New York: Routledge, 2015), ix.

18. Ko and Ko, *Aphro-Ism*, 50; Sincere Kirabo, "Three Ways Black Veganism Challenges White Supremacy (Unlike Conventional Veganism)," Black Youth Project, October 23, 2017, http://blackyouthproject.com/three-ways-black -veganism-challenges-white-supremacy-unlike-conventional-veganism/.

19. Howard Thurman, *Jesus and the Disinherited* (Boston: Beacon Press, 1996), 18.

20. Rogers, *Compassion in Practice*, 21.

21. Jesus articulates the third way in the Sermon on the Mount, Matthew 5–7.

22. Ko and Ko, *Aphro-Ism*, 53.

23. Michael Omi and Howard Winant, *Racial Formation in the United States*, 3rd ed. (New York: Routledge, 2014), 105.

24. Ibid., 110.

25. Ibid., 106. Omi and Winant do not argue that race is a transcendent category that stands above other axes of difference such as class and gender; rather, they assume the self-evident truth of intersectional marginalization. They point to the work of Patricia Hill Collins in *Black Feminist Thought*, particularly the chapter "Rethinking Black Women's Activism," as a key text

that describes the social organization within which intersecting oppressions of race, gender, and class originate, develop, and are contained.

26. Ibid., 106.

27. Ibid., 109, 125.

28. Emilie M. Townes, *Womanist Ethics and the Cultural Production of Evil* (New York: Palgrave Macmillan, 2007), 16.

29. Ibid., 21, 22.

30. This recipe is my adaptation of the red beans and rice recipe developed by Roberto Martin, *Vegan Cooking for Carnivores*, illustrated ed. (Grand Central Life & Style, 2013).

Chapter 1. Transatlantic Soul

1. Ibrahima Seck, *Bouki Fait Gombo* (New Orleans: University of New Orleans Press, 2014).

2. Ivone Gebara, *Longing for Running Water: Ecofeminism and Liberation* (Minneapolis, MN: Fortress Press, 1999), 25.

3. Mignolo and Walsh, *On Decoloniality*, 148.

4. Gebara, *Longing for Running Water*, 26.

5. Melanie Harris, *Ecowomanism: African American Women and Earth-Honoring Faiths* (New York: Orbis Books, 2017), 28.

6. Ibid., 27.

7. Judith Carney and Richard Nicholas Rosomoff, *In the Shadow of Slavery: Africa's Botanical Legacy in the Atlantic World* (Berkeley: University of California Press, 2011), 10, 14, 7, 25.

8. Jessica B. Harris, *High on the Hog: A Culinary Journey from Africa to America*, 1st U.S. ed. (New York: Bloomsbury, 2011), 10, 11.

9. Ibid., 14. Harris notes that yams often represented the continuity of new life because new yams grow from old ones.

10. Ibid., 11.

11. Ibid., 17. It is also worth noting that the English word "okra" is a descendant from the Igbo language of Nigeria, where the plant is called *okuru*. The French word for okra is *gombo*, which has a clear relationship to the Louisiana variation of the word, "gumbo," of which okra is a primary ingredient.

12. Ibid., 17.

13. Stephen Behrendt, "Ecology, Seasonality, and the Transatlantic Slave Trade," in *Soundings in Atlantic History*, ed. Bernard Bailyn and Patricia L. Denault (Cambridge, MA: Harvard University Press, 2009), 45.

14. Harris, *High on the Hog*, 33.

15. Ibid., 68.

16. Ibid., 69, 105.

17. Ibid., 65.

18. Ibid., 74, 76.

19. "Who Was James Hemings?," James Hemings Society, http://james hemingssociety.org/james-hemings/.

20. Psyche A. Williams-Forson, *Building Houses out of Chicken Legs: Black Women, Food, and Power* (Chapel Hill: University of North Carolina Press, 2006), 50. "Coon" is a derogatory term for "sneaky Negro," and in the South it was "common sense" to believe that coons steal chickens.

21. Ibid., 66.

22. Ibid., 43.

23. "Birth of a Nation Opens," History.com, http://www.history.com/this-day-in-history/birth-of-a-nation-opens.

24. Conrad Pitcher, "D. W. Griffith's Controversial Film, *The Birth of a Nation*," *Magazine of History* 13, no. 3 (Spring 1999): 50.

25. Ibid., 51.

26. Ibid.

27. Harris, *High on the Hog*, 104, quoting R. Q. Mallard, *Plantation Life before Emancipation* (Richmond: Whittet & Shepperson, 1892).

28. Williams-Forson, *Building Houses*, 80.

29. Ibid., 94.

30. Ibid., 95.

31. Frederick Douglass Opie, *Hog & Hominy: Soul Food from Africa to America*, Arts & Traditions of the Table (New York: Columbia University Press, 2008), 123, 124.

32. Ibid., 132.

33. Ibid., 159.

34. Williams-Forson, *Building Houses*, 138, 140.

35. Ibid., 140.

36. Joe Feagin, *The White Racial Frame: Centuries of Racial Framing and Counter-Framing*, 2nd ed. (New York: Routledge, 2013), 3.

37. Alice Walker, *In Search of Our Mothers' Gardens: Womanist Prose*, repr. ed. (Orlando, FL: Mariner Books, 2003).

38. Townes, *Womanist Ethics*, 47.

39. Ibid.

40. Harris, *High on the Hog*, 71, 146.

41. Ibid., 84.

42. Williams-Forson, *Building Houses*, 68.

43. Ibid., 68.

44. Townes, *Womanist Ethics*, 36.

45. Williams-Forson, *Building Houses*, 110.

46. Donovan O. Schaefer, *Religious Affects: Animality, Evolution, and Power* (Durham, NC: Duke University Press, 2015), 8.

47. Ibid., 73.

48. Opie, *Hog and Hominy*, 173.

49. Rogers, *Compassion in Practice*, 77.

50. Ibid., 78.

51. This recipe is adapted from Bryant Terry, *Vegan Soul Kitchen: Fresh, Healthy, and Creative African-American Cuisine* (Cambridge, MA: Da Capo Press, 2009), 4.

Chapter 2. Food Pyramid Scheme

1. Gottlieb and Joshi, *Food Justice*, 18.

2. Eric Holt Giménez, "Overcoming the Barrier of Racism in Our Capitalist Food System," Food First, March 19, 2018, https://foodfirst.org/publication/overcoming-the-barrier-of-racism-in-our-capitalist-food-system/.

3. Charlie LeDuff, "At a Slaughterhouse, Some Things Never Die; Who Kills, Who Cuts, Who Bosses Can Depend on Race," *New York Times*, June 16, 2000, sec. U.S., https://www.nytimes.com/2000/06/16/us/slaughterhouse -some-things-never-die-who-kills-who-cuts-who-bosses-can-depend.html.

4. Coalition of Immokalee Workers, "About CIW," http://ciw-online.org/ about/.

5. Coalition of Immokalee Workers, "Anti-slavery Campaign," http:// ciw-online.org/slavery/.

6. The term "food sovereignty" emerged in 2009 from within the food movement. Food sovereignty calls for food systems to change on the basis of rights, entitlements, structural reforms, and the redistribution of land, water, and other resources. This term is increasingly popular among food justice–seeking communities.

7. US Department of Agriculture, *USDA Celebrates 150 Years*, December 31, 2012, http://www.usda.gov/wps/portal/usda/usdahome?navid=USDA150.

8. Gottlieb and Joshi, *Food Justice*, 76.

9. Ibid.

10. Michael Pollan, "Farmer in Chief," *New York Times*, October 12, 2008, http://www.nytimes.com/2008/10/12/magazine/12policy-t.html.

11. Gottlieb and Joshi, *Food Justice*, 80.

12. Ibid., 81, 82.

13. Pollan, "Farmer in Chief."

14. Dan Imhoff, *Foodfight: The Citizen's Guide to a Food and Farm Bill* (Berkeley: University of California Press, 2007), 23.

15. Marion Nestle, *Food Politics: How the Food Industry Influences Nutrition and Health*, rev. and expanded ed., California Studies in Food and Culture 3 (Berkeley: University of California Press, 2007), 99.

16. Ibid., 99.

17. Ibid., 100.

18. Glenn Greenwald, "The FBI's Hunt for Two Missing Piglets Reveals the Federal Cover-Up of Barbaric Factory Farms," *Intercept* (blog), October

5, 2017, https://theintercept.com/2017/10/05/factory-farms-fbi-missing
-piglets-animal-rights-glenn-greenwald/.

19. Ibid.

20. Karin Brulliard, "USDA Abruptly Purges Animal Welfare Information from Its Website," *Washington Post*, February 3, 2017, sec. Animalia,
https://www.washingtonpost.com/news/animalia/wp/2017/02/03/the
-usda-abruptly-removes-animal-welfare-information-from-its-website/.

21. Nestle, *Food Politics*, 101.

22. Robert Paarlberg, *Food Politics: What Everyone Needs to Know*, 2nd ed.
(New York: Oxford University Press, 2013), 105, 107.

23. Vincent H. Smith, "Crony Farmers," *US News & World Report*, January 14, 2016, https://www.usnews.com/opinion/economic-intelligence/
articles/2016-01-14/farm-subsidies-are-crony-capitalism.

24. Debbie Weingarten, "Why Are America's Farmers Killing Themselves in
Record Numbers?," *The Guardian*, December 6, 2017, sec. US news, http://
www.theguardian.com/us-news/2017/dec/06/why-are-americas-farmers
-killing-themselves-in-record-numbers.

25. Wendy LiKamWa McIntosh, "Suicide Rates by Occupational
Group—17 States, 2012," *MMWR: Morbidity and Mortality Weekly Report* 65
(2016), https://doi.org/10.15585/mmwr.mm6525a1.

26. Weingarten, "Why Are America's Farmers?"

27. Waymon R. Hinson and Edward Robinson, "'We Didn't Get Nothing':
The Plight of Black Farmers," *Journal of African American Studies* 12, no. 3
(2008): 288.

28. Elsadig Elsheikh, "Race and Corporate Power in the US Food System:
Examining the Farm Bill," Food First, June 6, 2016, https://foodfirst.org/
publication/race-and-corporate-power-in-the-us-food-system-examining-the
-farm-bill/.

29. Hinson and Robinson, "'We Didn't Get Nothing,'" 291.

30. Ibid., 293.

31. Elsheikh, "Race and Corporate Power."

32. Tadlock Cowan and Jody Feder, "The Pigford Cases: USDA Settlement
of Discrimination Suits by Black Farmers," Congressional Research Service,
May 29, 2013, http://nationalaglawcenter.org/wp-content/uploads/assets/
crs/RS20430.pdf.

33. Elsheikh, "Race and Corporate Power."

34. Raj Patel, *Stuffed and Starved: Markets, Power and the Hidden Battle for the
World Food System*, 1st Canadian ed. (Toronto: HarperCollins, 2007), 81.

35. Ibid., 95, 97.

36. Ibid., 97.

37. Nora McKeon, *Food Security Governance: Empowering Communities, Regu-
lating Corporations*, 1st ed. (New York: Routledge, 2015), 20, 36.

38. "Public Research, Private Gain: Corporate Influence over University
Agricultural Research," Food and Water Watch, Washington, DC, April

2012, https://www.foodandwaterwatch.org/sites/default/files/Public%20
Research%20Private%20Gain%20Report%20April%202012.pdf.

39. Ibid.

40. McKeon, *Food Security Governance*, 40, 41.

41. Patel, *Stuffed and Starved*, 41.

42. Katharine Child, "Farmer Suicides Soar as Worst Drought in Decades
Drives Them to Ruin," *Rand Daily Mail*, April 2017, https://www.businesslive
.co.za/rdm/news/2017–04–19-farmer-suicides-soar-as-worst-drought-in
-decades-drives-them-to-ruin/.

43. Patel, *Stuffed and Starved*, 26.

44. Omi and Winant, *Racial Formation*, 125.

45. Ibid., 128.

46. Robert D. Bullard, "Anatomy of Environmental Racism and the Environmental Justice Movement," in *Confronting Environmental Racism: Voices from
the Grassroots*, ed. Robert D. Bullard (Boston: South End Press, 1993), 15.

47. Ibid., 17.

48. Ibid., 18.

49. Ibid., 18.

50. Ibid., 23.

51. Jim Vallette, "Larry Summers' War against the Earth," Global Policy Forum, 1999, https://archive.globalpolicy.org/socecon/envronmt/summers
.htm.

52. Nestle, *Food Politics*, 146.

53. Ibid., 147.

54. Stacey M. Floyd-Thomas, *Mining the Motherlode: Methods in Womanist
Ethics* (Cleveland, OH: Pilgrim Press, 2006), 10.

55. Nestle, *Food Politics*, 149, 148. For an example of one such image, see
148.

56. Ibid., 148.

57. Ibid., 155.

58. Collins O. Airhihenbuwa, *Healing Our Differences: The Crisis of Global
Health and the Politics of Identity* (Lanham, MD: Rowman & Littlefield, 2006),
108.

59. Mark Winne, *Closing the Food Gap: Resetting the Table in the Land of Plenty*
(Boston: Beacon Press, 2009), 86.

60. Ibid., xviii; "USDA Definitions of Food Security," September 2014,
http://www.ers.usda.gov/topics/food-nutrition-assistance/food-security
-in-the-us/definitions-of-food-security.aspx. Low food security is defined as
a diet of reduced quality, variety, or desirability with little or no indication
of reduced food intake. Very low food security is defined as multiple indica-
tions of disrupted eating patterns and reduced food intake.

61. "Fact Sheet: Poverty and Hunger among African Americans," Bread
for the World Institute, February 2011, http://www.bread.org/what-we-do/
resources/fact-sheets/african-american-poverty.pdf.

62. Prior to the introduction of Electronic Benefits Transfer (EBT) cards in 1988, food stamps were distributed as a form of paper currency. See "Supplemental Nutrition Assistance Program (SNAP)," https://web.archive.org/web/20160812204314/http://www.fns.usda.gov/snap/short-history-snap.

63. Harris, *High on the Hog*, 17.

64. Laurel Wamsley, "Tyson Foods Fires 7 Plant Managers over Betting Ring on Workers Getting COVID-19," NPR.org, December 16, 2020, https://www.npr.org/sections/coronavirus-live-updates/2020/12/16/947275866/tyson-foods-fires-7-plant-managers-over-betting-ring-on-workers-getting-covid-19.

65. Eric Holt-Gimenez and Raj Patel, *Food Rebellions: Crisis and the Hunger for Justice* (Food First Books, 2012), 86.

66. This recipe is adapted from Terry, *Vegan Soul Kitchen*, 91.

Chapter 3. Being Human as Praxis

1. Thurman, *Jesus and the Disinherited*, 13.

2. I use the terms "nonhuman nature" and "nonhuman animals" as a way to remind us that we human beings are a part of and within nature. We do not transcend nature or exist outside of nature. Likewise, we are also members of the animal kingdom and therefore must think theologically about our relationship with other animals.

3. Dwight N. Hopkins, *Being Human: Race, Culture, and Religion* (Minneapolis: Fortress Press, 2005), 4.

4. Howard Thurman, *With Head and Heart: The Autobiography of Howard Thurman* (San Diego: Mariner Books, 1981), 20, emphasis added.

5. Raj Patel and Jason W. Moore, *A History of the World in Seven Cheap Things: A Guide to Capitalism, Nature, and the Future of the Planet* (Oakland: University of California Press, 2017), 22.

6. Ibid., 46.

7. Rene Descartes, *Discourse on Method and Meditations on First Philosophy*, trans. Donald A. Cress, 4th ed. (Indianapolis: Hackett Publishing Company, 1999).

8. Patel and Moore, *A History*, 53.

9. Ibid., 192.

10. J. Kameron Carter, "Humanity in African American Theology," in *Oxford Handbook of African American Theology*, ed. Katie G. Cannon and Anthony B. Pinn (New York: Oxford University Press, 2014), 176.

11. Ibid., 176, 177.

12. Thurman, *Jesus and the Disinherited*, 33.

13. Michael Lipka and Gregory Smith, "White Evangelical Approval of Trump Slips, but Eight-in-Ten Say They Would Vote for Him," Pew Re-

search Center (blog), July 1, 2020, https://www.pewresearch.org/fact
-tank/2020/07/01/white-evangelical-approval-of-trump-slips-but-eight-in
-ten-say-they-would-vote-for-him/.

14. Spiegel, *The Dreaded Comparison*, 22.

15. Emilie M. Townes, *Breaking the Fine Rain of Death: African American Health Issues and a Womanist Ethic of Care* (New York: Continuum, 1998), 88.

16. Ibid., 82, 83.

17. Ibid., 51.

18. James Baldwin, "An Open Letter to My Sister, Miss Angela Davis," *New York Review of Books*, January 7, 1971, http://www.nybooks.com/articles/archives/1971/jan/07/an-open-letter-to-my-sister-miss-angela-davis/.

19. Ko and Ko, *Aphro-Ism*, 45.

20. Ibid., emphasis added.

21. Frantz Fanon, *The Wretched of the Earth*, trans. Richard Philcox, reprint ed. (New York: Grove Press, 2005), 7.

22. Ko and Ko, *Aphro-Ism*, 47.

23. Ibid., 46.

24. David A. Nibert, *Animal Rights / Human Rights: Entanglements of Oppression and Liberation* (Lanham, MD: Rowman & Littlefield, 2002), 4.

25. "Illegal Wildlife Trade," World Wildlife Fund, http://www.worldwildlife.org/threats/illegal-wildlife-trade.

26. Nibert, *Animal Rights*, 14.

27. Ibid.

28. I should also note that the scope of my constructive project is not intended to be comprehensive; rather, it is focused on the God-human relationship relative to environmental ethics and, more specifically, food injustice.

29. Willie James Jennings, *The Christian Imagination: Theology and the Origins of Race* (New Haven, CT: Yale University Press, 2011), 63.

30. Ellen F. Davis, *Scripture, Culture, and Agriculture: An Agrarian Reading of the Bible* (New York: Cambridge University Press, 2009), 43. A healthy religious imagination is essential for enabling people to see the world both as it is and as it could be. Davis writes: "Imagination is the means whereby writers with diverse gifts may enable their communities literally to re-member, to work toward their own wholeness, a goal that can be achieved only by claiming membership . . . in the wholeness of the Holiness of the Creation" (16). Walter Brueggemann argues for a liturgical and poetic interpretation of Genesis 1 in *Genesis, Interpretation: A Bible Commentary for Teaching and Preaching* (Atlanta: John Knox, 1982).

31. Davis, *Scripture*, 150.

32. Theodore Hiebert, "The Human Vocation: Origins and Transformations in Christian Tradition," in *Christianity and Ecology*, ed. Dieter T. Hessel

and Rosemary Radford Ruether (Cambridge, MA: Harvard University Press, 2000), 140.

33. Davis, *Scripture*, 29.

34. Ibid., 56.

35. Karen Baker-Fletcher, *Sisters of Dust, Sisters of Spirit: Womanist Wordings on God and Creation* (Minneapolis: Fortress Press, 1998), 18.

36. Ibid.

37. Townes, *Breaking the Fine Rain*, 25, 24.

38. Baker-Fletcher, *Sisters of Dust*, 113.

39. M. Shawn Copeland, *Enfleshing Freedom: Body, Race, and Being* (Minneapolis: Fortress Press, 2009), 58–59.

40. Ibid., 60.

41. Ibid., 94.

42. To be clear, there may be instances where harming or killing a nonhuman animal is unfortunately necessary such as for the protection of one's life from danger or death. Generally speaking, for most people these instances will rarely if ever occur.

43. Copeland, *Enfleshing Freedom*, 94, 95.

44. Hopkins, *Being Human*, 5.

45. Baker-Fletcher, *Sisters of Dust*, 19.

46. Biblical scholar J. Richard Middleton claims that Hebrew Bible scholars have come to a virtual consensus on the functional interpretation of the *imago Dei*. This consensus is based on a combination of two factors: the literary context of Genesis 1:1–2:3 and attention to the ancient Near Eastern background of the *imago Dei*. According to this consensus, we humans "image" God in the ways that we have been called and authorized to "share in God's rule or administration of the earth's resources and creatures." J. Richard Middleton, *The Liberating Image: The Imago Dei in Genesis 1* (Grand Rapids, MI: Brazos Press, 2005), 27.

47. Peter J. Paris, *Virtues and Values: The African and African American Experience* (Minneapolis: Augsburg Fortress Press, 2004), 135.

48. Tyler Tully, "The Extraction of Flesh in Trump's America: Extending Environmental Racism beyond Toxic Encroachment," paper presented at the American Academy of Religion conference, San Diego, CA, 2019.

49. Karen Warren, *Ecofeminist Philosophy: A Western Perspective on What It Is and Why It Matters* (Lanham, MD: Rowman and Littlefield, 2000), 47, emphasis added.

50. William Vitek and Wes Jackson, eds., *Rooted in the Land: Essays on Community and Place* (New Haven, CT: Yale University Press, 1996). This anthology contains contributions from Wendell Berry, Walter Brueggemann, and John Cobb, among others who endorse a bioregionalist approach to earth care.

51. Lisa H. Sideris, *Environmental Ethics, Ecological Theology, and Natural Selection* (New York: Columbia University Press, 2003), 258.

52. Copeland, *Enfleshing Freedom*, 94.

Chapter 4. Tasting Freedom

1. Steven W. Manskar, Marjorie Suchocki, and Diana L. Hynson, eds., *A Perfect Love: Understanding John Wesley's "A Plain Account of Christian Perfection"* (Nashville, TN: Discipleship Resources, 2004).

2. Peter J. Paris, *The Spirituality of African Peoples* (Minneapolis: Fortress Press, 1994), 133.

3. Ibid., 134.

4. Ibid., 144.

5. Ibid., 146, 147.

6. Ibid., 152.

7. Henning Steinfeld et al., "Livestock's Long Shadow," Food and Agriculture Organization of the United Nations, 2006, 272, http://www.fao.org/docrep/010/a0701e/a0701e00.HTM.

8. Anne Bower, "Recipes for History: The National Council of Negro Women's Five Historical Cookbooks," in *African American Foodways: Explorations of History and Culture*, ed. Anne Bower (Urbana: University of Illinois Press, 2007), 153; Sue Bailey Thurman and Anne Bower, eds., *The Historical Cookbook of the American Negro*, 2nd ed. (Boston: Beacon Press, 2000).

9. Michael W. Twitty, *The Cooking Gene: A Journey through African American Culinary History in the Old South* (New York: Amistad, 2018), 11.

10. Laura Hobgood-Oster, "Does Christian Hospitality Require That We Eat Meat?," in *A Faith Embracing All Creatures: Addressing Commonly Asked Questions about Christian Care for Animals*, ed. Tripp York and Andy Alexis-Baker (Eugene, OR: Cascade Books, 2012), 78.

11. Ibid., 87.

12. Annika Spalde and Pelle Strindlund, "Doesn't Jesus Treat Animals as Property?," in York and Alexis-Baker, *A Faith Embracing*, 103, 104, 106.

13. Stephen Webb, "Didn't Jesus Eat Lamb? The Last Supper and the Case of the Missing Meat," in York and Alexis-Baker, *A Faith Embracing*, 53. The theological significance of lamb being absent from the table is important to note: Webb writes that the "Lord's Supper enacted a logic of sacrificial substitution that rendered the lamb not just redundant but insufferable" (62). In other words, Jesus becomes the ultimate sacrifice that frees both human and nonhuman animals from death and oppression.

14. Alexis-Baker, "Didn't Jesus Eat Fish?," in York and Alexis-Baker, *A Faith Embracing*, 65, 69.

15. "Adults' Daily Protein Intake Much More Than Recommended," *NCHStats: A Blog of the National Center for Health Statistics*, March 2010, http://

nchstats.com/2010/03/03/adults%e2%80%99-daily-protein-intake-much
-more-than-recommended/.

16. Winston J. Craig, "Health Effects of Vegan Diets," *American Journal
of Clinical Nutrition* 89, no. 5 (May 2009): 1627S–33S, https://doi.org/
10.3945/ajcn.2009.26736N.

17. Neo-Kantian philosopher Christine Korsgaard has advanced a very
reasonable argument that if human beings are able to gather animal products such as eggs, dairy, and wool in ways that did not inhibit the ability of
the animal to live a good life, meaning that we would be responsible for
providing living conditions wherein they are able to lead something reasonably like their own sort of life, such actions could be morally permissible.
As I have argued, vegetarianism does not address the racial logics latent in
the human/animal divide, a weakness when compared to veganism. But for
those unable to practice veganism, Korsgaard makes a compelling argument
for principled vegetarianism. See Christine Korsgaard, "Fellow Creatures:
Kantian Ethics and Our Duties to Animals," in *The Tanner Lectures on Human Values*, ed. Grethe B. Peterson (Salt Lake City: University of Utah Press,
2005), 102–3; Korsgaard, "Exploiting Animals: A Philosophical Protest," *AV
Magazine*, Fall 2009.

18. Economic Policy Institute, "The State of Working America: Poverty
Rate, by Race and Ethnicity, and Age, 2013," Economic Policy Institute blog,
2013, http://www.stateofworkingamerica.org/.

19. Charles C. Camosy, *For Love of Animals: Christian Ethics, Consistent Action*
(Cincinnati, OH: Franciscan Media, 2013), 93.

20. Matthew Halteman, "Compassionate Eating as Care of Creation," Hu-
mane Society of the United States, 2008, 25.

21. Camosy, *For Love of Animals*, 94.

22. "Community Services Unlimited : Serving the People Body and Soul,"
http://csuinc.org/.

23. "Food Empowerment Project | Because Your Food Choices Can
Change the World," http://www.foodispower.org/.

24. United Nations, Food and Agriculture Organization, "The Female
Face of Farming," Infographic, Food and Agriculture Organization of the
United Nations, http://www.fao.org/gender/infographic/en/.

25. "Economic Empowerment of Women: Progress Report on the Proposed
African Bank for Women and Promotion of Women Entrepreneurship,"
United Nations Economic Commission for Africa, http://www.uneca.org/
cfm1995/pages/economic-empowerment-women-progress-report-proposed
-african-bank-women-and-promotion.

26. Monica M. White, "'A Pig and a Garden': Fannie Lou Hamer and the
Freedom Farms Cooperative," *Food and Foodways* 25, no. 1 (January 2017):
20–39, https://doi.org/10.1080/07409710.2017.1270647.

27. Ibid.

28. Rob Nixon, *Slow Violence and the Environmentalism of the Poor* (Cambridge, MA: Harvard University Press, 2013), 2.

29. White, "'A Pig and a Garden.'"

30. Eric Holt-Gimenez and Raj Patel, *Food Rebellions: Crisis and the Hunger for Justice* (Oakland, CA: Food First Books, 2012), 86.

31. "Home Page BCFSN," Black Church Food Security Network, n.d., http://blackchurchfoodsecurity.net/.

32. Ibid.

33. "Mission: Los Angeles Food Policy Council," Los Angeles Food Policy Council, http://goodfoodla.org/about/mission/.

34. "UFW: Our Vision," UFW: The Official Web Page of the United Farm Workers of America, 2015, http://www.ufw.org/_page.php?menu=about&inc=about_vision.html.

35. Camosy, *For Love of Animals*, 95.

36. Ibid., 92.

37. A. Breeze Harper, "Social Justice Beliefs and Addiction to Uncompassionate Consumption: Food for Thought," in *Sistah Vegan: Black Female Vegans Speak on Food, Identity, Health, and Society*, ed. A. Breeze Harper (New York: Lantern Books, 2010).

38. "About Beyond Meat: The Future of Protein,", http://beyondmeat.com/about. The conversation between Ethan and me took place on June 5, 2015.

39. "Food and Faith Convening: Duke Sanford World Food Policy Center," November 2018, https://wfpc.sanford.duke.edu/projects/food-and-faith-convening-november-2018.

40. "The Movement to Turn Church Land into Farmland," Civil Eats, June 11, 2018, https://civileats.com/2018/06/11/the-movement-to-turn-church-land-into-farmland/.

41. Elaine Nogueira-Godsey, "Towards a Decological Praxis," *Horizontes decoloniales / Decolonial Horizons* 5 (2019): 73–98.

42. Dianne D. Glave, *Rooted in the Earth: Reclaiming the African American Environmental Heritage*, 1st ed. (Chicago: Lawrence Hill Books, 2010), 4.

43. Christopher Carter, "Blood in the Soil: The Racial, Racist, and Religious Dimensions of Environmentalism," in *The Bloomsbury Handbook of Religion and Nature: The Elements*, ed. Laura Hobgood and Whitney Bauman (London: Bloomsbury Academic, 2018), 45–61.

44. Leah Penniman and Karen Washington, *Farming While Black: Soul Fire Farm's Practical Guide to Liberation on the Land* (White River Junction, VT: Chelsea Green Publishing, 2018), 1.

45. Ibid., 3.

46. "Soul Fire Farm," Soul Fire Farm, http://www.soulfirefarm.org/.

47. Given the nature of the text, my exploration of the work of Wangari Maathai is limited in scope. I primarily focus on the religious and social dimensions of her work. This brief analysis does not do justice to her amaz-

ing contributions to the world. For more information about her work, see Wangari Maathai, *The Green Belt Movement: Sharing the Approach and the Experience* (New York: Lantern Books, 2003); Maathai, *Unbowed: A Memoir* (New York: Anchor, 2007).

48. "Our History," Green Belt Movement blog, 2018, http://www.green beltmovement.org/who-we-are/our-history.

49. Wangari Maathai, *Replenishing the Earth: Spiritual Values for Healing Ourselves and the World* (New York: Doubleday Religion, 2010), 14.

50. Rogers, *Compassion in Practice*, 117.

Conclusion

1. Ashcroft, Griffiths, and Tiffin, *Post-colonial Studies*, 73.

2. Fanon, *The Wretched*, 11.

3. Aimé Césaire, *Discourse on Colonialism*, trans. Joan Pinkham (New York: Monthly Review Press, 2001), 52, emphasis added.

Index

Supplemental Nutrition Assistance Program (SNAP), 63, 139, 172n62

theological anthropology, 12, 18–19, 88, 90–91, 96–98, 116, 119, 163; Black soul and, 161; coloniality and, 95, 107, 110; decolonial, 90, 103–107, 110–113, 118–120, 128–129, 134, 146, 155; farmworker injustice and, 58; human/animal tension and, 100–101, 103; soulfull eating and, 128; veganism and, 134; white supremacy and, 98–99, 103, 158, 161. *See also* Christianity
Thurman, Howard, 13, 87–89, 95, 104, 118, 120, 131
Thurman, Sue Bailey, 125, 131
Tometi, Opal, 9
Townes, Emilie, 17, 46–47, 49–50, 97, 109–110
triangle trade, 29
Trump, Donald, 15, 95
Tuskegee syphilis study, 97–98
Twitty, Michael, 125, 132

United Farm Workers, 144
United States Department of Agriculture (USDA), 60–69, 85; Black farmers and, 66–69

veganism, 8, 14, 19, 136, 176n17; agricultural workers and, 145–146; author's transition to, 19–21; black veganism (*see* black veganism); Christian morality and, 134; environmental benefits of, 147–148; plant-based meat alternatives, 147–148; vegan recipes (*see* recipes). *See also* black veganism
Via Campesina, 142
virtuous practices. *See* moral virtue

Walker, Alice, 46–47
Warren, Karen, 117
Wartman, Kristin, 5
Washington, George, 33
Washington, Karen, 150
watermelon, 29–30, 48, 154–156, 155–156
Wernette, Leslie, 76
Wesley, John, 123
West African agriculture, 26–30, 47–48; triangular trade and, 29
Whatley, Booker T., 151
Wheatley, Phyllis, 46
white Christians, 88, 95, 100, 105, 113–116, 129, 161
whiteness, 8, 75, 101, 103, 120; coloniality and, 158; decentering of, 12, 106, 113–114, 117, 120, 128–129, 136, 155, 158, 163; decolonization and, 88, 149; food systems and, 75; theological anthropology and, 90, 103
white supremacy, 8, 52, 94, 130, 163; Christianity and, 93–95, 98–99, 113, 116, 129; coloniality and, 4, 88, 129–130, 159; environmental justice and, 90; human/animal divide and, 13, 100–101, 120, 128–130, 161; human rights and, 159; soul food as resistance to, 12, 156, 163; theological anthropology and, 98–99, 103, 158, 161
Whitney Plantation, 23–24
Williams-Forson, Psyche, 35–36, 45, 50
Winant, Howard, 15–16
Winne, Mark, 80–81
Winter, Sylvia, 11
World Bank, 69–71, 77–78
World Trade Organization (WTO), 60, 70–71, 73, 77, 85, 138, 143

Zip Coon image, 35–37, 39, 155, 168n20

CHRISTOPHER CARTER is an assistant professor of theology and religious studies at the University of San Diego. He is also a pastor within the United Methodist Church and has served churches in Battle Creek, Michigan, and in Torrance and Compton, California.

The University of Illinois Press
is a founding member of the
Association of University Presses.

_____ ᵎ

Composed in 10.25/14 ITC New Baskerville Std
with Frutiger LT Std display
by Lisa Connery
at the University of Illinois Press
Manufactured by Sheridan Books, Inc.

University of Illinois Press
1325 South Oak Street
Champaign, IL 61820-6903
www.press.uillinois.edu